SURVIVING HELL

SHEREE COLEMAN

STORYTELLER BOOKS, LLC

CONTENTS

I would like to dedicate this book to my children. You are the reason I strive to be a better version of myself.

PROLOGUE

Droplets of rain shimmered and slid down the coffee shop windows that encased the busy people scurrying for their cup of sanity. Her cold hands gently wrapped around her own steaming mug absorbing the warmth the overpriced coffee so freely gave off. Hesitation weighed in her throat. She knew what she was called to do, but every part of her wanted to pull away; to hide. Was she really ready to step out; to step up; to reveal a story sometimes so dark that not even demons dared draw near. Afterall, if her dark tale could make the demonic forces cheer with glee, what makes her think that humans would want to dip their minds into the black abyss of her story?

Lost in a self-absorbed coma, she finally woke from her stupor to see a worn down woman with blood shot sunken eyes staring back at her. The woman stood just inside the double glass doors that invited people inside to become momentarily lost in the hippy chic world of peace, love, and java. Her dingy brown trench coat dripped from the rain that had just previously soaked it. The sharp protruding cheek bones revealed that a steady stream of solid food had been absent for months. Her stringy hair was glued to her scalp, but it was the eyes that struck a nerve. They were the eyes of a dead woman walking. The woman standing frozen in place was lost in a whirlwind of torment that made the storm outside seem like child's play.

In that moment she remembered why she said yes to come to the coffee shop to meet a stranger. She felt that all too familiar pain that only those who have traveled down hell's path know. It was in that same moment that she knew she must lay aside her selfish nature to reach out her hand to another lost soul. She could not hide her story and call herself spiritual. She could not pretend that shame, guilt, and remorse were not imbedded into her background and claim to be in recovery. No matter what others may say, or think her duty was to reveal her story in the hopes that someone somewhere would be made the better for it. She rose from the oversized chair, like leaving a cushy cocoon, to greet the woman still frozen at the doors. Her voice crackled a response as she looked deep into the eyes of the woman standing a few feet before her. "Hello. I assume you are Carol."

Pushing a strand of hair from her wrinkled forehead, the woman simply said, "Yes. Yes I'm Carol. You must be Faith."

Motioning for Carol to sit on the chair next to her, Faith braced herself to tell a story she had run from, hid from, and now could not escape from. "Sit please, and don't let my name fool you. I'm no Bible-thumper. I'm just a screwed up lady who clings to a God of my understanding. I'm not going to preach at you. You're safe here. The chair is cozy trust me. I always sit in these chairs when I come here 'cause their soft cloth cushions make me feel like I'm a little kid sitting in the adults' chair. I don't know, I just like how safe they make me feel."

A wave of relief fell over Carol's expression easing the stern cynical mask she came in wearing. "Good to hear, 'cause I'm not into religion. Never did nothing for me."

"Neither am I."

Carol took off her old coat and sat down. Her cold blue eyes bore into the woman who chose to see her. "I was told you could help me."

Faith inhaled the flavored steam from her coffee and let a sigh escape her lips. Slowly, a smile spread across her face. One screwed up person helping another is the best thing in the world. The once damned helping the damned is the greatest irony in life. "I don't know if I can help you. All I can do is share my story. What you do with it is on you."

"Well, I'm here. So, whatcha got that I haven't heard a thousand times before?"

Faith groaned internally. *Great, another one. I'm gonna rip open old wounds for some cynical critic who can barely walk in a straight line.* Voices of old-timers spoke in her head. *Doesn't matter what she does with the information. What matters is that you share your human experience just as others shared with you. It's your obligation to all who helped you. This meeting isn't about you. It's about recovery. Besides, remember the mess you were. Don't pretend you weren't a disaster tearing through life.*

A long pause held in the air between two strangers that fate had brought together. Neither woman could fully understand why they shared this time and space. To any onlooker the pair could not have been more mismatched. By appearance they had nothing in common. One woman seemed to have life together. Nails done. Hair blonde, long, and well groomed. Clothes ironed and perfectly matched. The other disheveled. Nails broken and the fingernail polish chipped. Brown hair matted, greasy and uncombed. Clothes wrinkled and unwashed. But it is not what is seen that connects the stories of souls. It is the unseen reality, the unspoken words between the experiences of strangers that fate strings together in the strangest of ways.

Faith drank from her cup. *One must do what one must do. It is the way among all who have travelled hell's path. No better way to beat hell back into the chasm it burst from than to snatch up one of its victims.*

Faith stared into her coffee watching the light reflect shapes in the cinnamon colored liquid. "I remember the day I woke up dead."

Carol stared blankly and fidgeted with her fingernails scraping at the left over polish. "Well that's a bit of a dramatic introduction. Don't ya think?"

Small chuckles gently shook Faith's shoulders. "My journey from hell is a bit on the dramatic side as it is for everyone facing their demons. Demons long unchained tend to be a bit dramatic when you attempt to not just bind them, but to eradicate them forever. Besides, I have a flare for the spectacularly dark, so why not indulge myself a little in this dark dramatic play we're in?"

Carol shifted uncomfortably in her seat crossing one leg over the other then switching. "Now you're talking about demons and hell. I thought you said you weren't a Bible-thumper, or are you one those Goth types?"

Faith eased back into her own chair, allowing the oversized cushion to swallow her. She held Carol's stare. "You don't have to be a preacher, or a Goth to believe in demons, but the demons I speak of are the ones of our own creation. The ones that emerge from the filth of our minds, from the ghosts of our memories we have refused to deal with."

Carol blinked and went back to her nervous fidgeting. "Oh, so you were saying that you woke up dead? I mean, how is that even possible? Were you in the hospital, or something?"

Faith waved her hand to dismiss Carol's question. "I don't mean physically dead. Don't get me wrong. I wanted death. I ached for it. But I was very much alive. I could walk. I could talk. I could even laugh on cue. Yet, inside I was a dead woman screaming to a dead world to come and save me. I was looking at my reflection that morning when I realized I couldn't do this anymore."

Carol eased into her chair. "You're right, you do have a flare for the dark side. Sure, hope your whole talk isn't like this. I may want to jump off a bridge by the time you're done. Anyway, you couldn't do what anymore?"

Faith's green eyes stared into Carol's faded and lifeless blue orbs. "Live."

WEB OF TORMENT

*B*lack waters. Black skies. No light. No sound. She was drifting in the abyss crying for someone to help her before she drowned. A small piece of driftwood kept her afloat, but her arms burned from exhaustion. She was slipping. Something moved the current beneath her. Her heart leapt into her throat. She went to scream, but no sound escaped. The water shifted all around her ankles, up her legs, her waist, her breast, and finally around her neck. She kicked her legs frantically, but her arms could no longer hold onto the splintering life raft and she slipped into the water. *No, no, no. Not yet. Help me. God help me.*

Her face looked up into the darkness resisting the water quickly closing in around her nostrils. That something moving the water slithered a slimy firm tentacle up her legs interlacing its arm around her leg. She could feel its weight pulling, tugging her further down into the water. Sea foam splashed across her, enveloped her. She stopped fighting. There was no point anymore. She was tired. She let go of the only life raft she knew. She fell back into the nothingness breathing in the fluid that would choke out life.

The alarm screamed inside Faith's murky dream. Rushing to turn off the noise, she felt her head throb to the pulse of her heart as the remnants of her all-too-familiar nightmare receded into memory. Last night's wine fermented in her mouth. She sat on the edge of her bed for a moment letting her toes gently touch the carpet. *Ug, why did I drink so much. Oh, well it's another day. No worries. No matter what happens today I can drink again tonight. I just have to get through the day and tonight I will enjoy my reward for not killing anyone.*

Standing up, Faith trudged her feet across the carpet to the bathroom. A quick flick of the switch brought fluorescent lights burning into her eyes. Movement caught her attention. Her reflection stood there, staring back at her. *Dear God I look like I got hit by a truck.*

Wrinkles and bags were beginning to gather around her eyes that were swimming in a sea of red. Ashy white skin held together a form of a woman that no longer knew anything about anything. She splashed cold water on her face. Grabbing the sides of the sink she tried to gather the strength to fight another day knowing full well that this day would end like all the other days—at the end of a bottle.

Swallowing aspirin and grabbing her makeup, Faith painted on the face that everyone knew, but that no one saw. She stood in front of the mirror staring at the stranger staring back at her. She saw her mouth move. She heard her voice whisper. She held no answer to the question that would spark a journey into a world that would wrap her into a web of torment before releasing her into a new dimension. "What am I doing?"

She looked at the stranger in the mirror. Her hands fingered and tugged at her hair. She was slip, slip, slipping into a whirl-wind. She tried to catch her thoughts, to study them, to stop them. Round and round they went where and when they would stop she had no clue. Minutes fly and there she stands—little girl lost in the chaos. Anger simmered; began to boil. It demanded release. Over and over anger swooped down over her.

She had to release it, or burn to ash from the inside out. She balled her fist. Tightened it until her nails dug into her palm. Release. She needed release. The thoughts wouldn't stop. They swung at her. She went to catch then missed. Her fist pulsated. Flames torched through her veins. Her reflection screamed. Her fists beat against her skull. Pain pounded into the grey matter of her tormented mind.

Pound. Bang. Boom. Fists against skull. Waters of relief rushed over the fires scorching in her veins. Tears of agony delicately dripped down her cheeks. "Make it stop. Someone make it stop." She whimpered. She begged. She pleaded.

Crumbling to the floor, exhausted, Faith trembled. Her head pulsed from the blows she inflicted upon herself. Her pounding of pain left no scar to be seen and left no bruise for eyes to question. She sat on the cold bathroom floor swimming in her liberation from the insanity that now surrounded her.

Why? Why was she like this? Where did the thoughts come from? Why did they come like machine gun fire? She felt crazy. She felt like her mind was splitting away from reality.

No matter what, time ticks on. It stops for no one; even when they're fracturing into a thousand pieces. Faith pulled herself up from the floor. Another look at the stranger. She combed her hair and wiped away her tears. Faith switched off the light and left the scene behind to become a memory to join the other memories of self-harm. It was just another episode of turmoil.

The clock on her phone told her time still wasn't waiting for anyone let alone a drunk fighting a hangover and possibly insanity, so she forced herself to pick up the pace. She put on her blue and white pants suit that always made her feel like a fierce business woman who could take down giants. Faith walked into her outdated kitchen whose cabinets were made during the 70's, and had floors that were a dingy brown tile that Faith had grown to dislike over the years. She made the black liquor that would offer some relief from the haze she had become accustomed to living in. A pack of cigarettes waited for her on the white counter. Without thinking, she grabbed a cigarette, a lighter, and stepped outside with her cup of coffee. Night still held onto the approaching morning while Faith lit her first cigarette of the day. In the distance, a lone bird began to sing its song. Tears welled in her eyes. *How long can I keep doing this? Maybe it's time to make a change. Maybe I should find a new job. Maybe we should move. Maybe I should just end this? End what? Your life? There you go again being dramatic. So, you have a hangover, it'll go away. Stop your whining and get on with the day.*

One of the alarms on Faith's phone told her that it was time to wake the kids. She welcomed the distraction that waking the kids would bring from the chaos haunting her mind. Before waking the kids Faith went to put the creamer away into the fridge. And there it was welcoming her. A cold beer. How it had survived last night before baffled her for a brief moment before the thought of drinking just one entered her mind.

Just one beer wouldn't hurt. It would take away the hangover better than coffee. Besides you've had a rough morning. A little beer will smooth things over. It always does.

Faith stood in her kitchen whispering to herself like a madman clinging to reality. "No, I can't. I swore to never drink in the morning."

What's one drink? No one will know.

"They will smell it on my breath."

That's what Listerine is for.

"I don't have any."

You have gum, don't you? That will work. Come on. It's just one drink.

"I do have gum. One beer won't hurt. I'm drinking it to take away the hangover, so that I can work better"

Go ahead. Open that ice cold beer.

I can't.

Who says?

I shouldn't.

Why not? Who is going to know?

A force unknown, but all too familiar possessed Faith. She reached for the beer, unscrewed the top, and heard that sweet sound of the bottle releasing air. Before she could argue, before she could think of any logical reason to throw away the beer, before she could stop, the bottle tipped into her mouth unleashing the cold contents that sent an immediate wave of warm release throughout her body. She didn't stop nursing the bottle until the beer was gone.

You see? You didn't die. Lightening didn't strike. So, what if you like to start your day with a little extra help to kickstart things? Lots of people do it.

Immediate guilt swept over Faith. "What have I done? What is wrong with me?"

Nothing is wrong with you. Lots of people start with a drink. They just don't talk about it.

No, normal people don't drink in the mornings.

Is anyone really normal? You have a job don't you? You're fine.

A third alarm on the phone reminded her that she had kids to wake up and a job to go to. "Shit! Now I'm running late."

Fumbling through her purse, she found the gum, grabbed two pieces, began chewing, and praying that the kids would not smell her sin. Going room to room, Faith woke the kids up for school all the while cursing herself for drinking that beer and at the same time for not having more in the fridge so she could have downed two beers instead of just the one.

She barged into her youngest, Mary's, room.

"Let's go! We are going to be late if ya'll don't get in gear."

"What about breakfast?" Faith's youngest stared up at her with innocent brown eyes. Sleep still hung on to her tightly as she sat up in the bed.

"Do y'all really need to eat?"

"Mom! Of course we do. We are growing children that need nutrition. Besides breakfast is the most important meal of the day. How else is my brain supposed to work? You always said I should never skip breakfast. You said..."

"Yes, I know what I said! Just like you to remember everything I have ever told you, but from what I can see you can never seem to remember when I tell you to clean your room."

"Mom, it IS clean. Just not your definition of clean. For example, I know where everything is."

"Oh, how I doubt that. For example, where are your socks?"

"Mom, that is beside the point."

Hurriedly, Faith walked away from her baby girl as she continued to babble on about her form of organization. "Find your socks and get your shoes on. We will grab breakfast at the corner store."

"Corner store again? Whatever happened to a real breakfast?" Athena, her oldest, stood in the long hallway ready for school. It was just like Athena to be up and ready before her mom came to her room. Her uniform perfectly pressed, white socks pulled up to the knees, and her overstuffed backpack hanging off one shoulder.

Faith knew her daughter was half joking, but the words stung just the same. Truth is that every morning was all about coping with a hangover. Cooking breakfast or putting out cereal and milk was just too much to deal with. This morning espe-cially. *Maybe tomorrow will be better. Maybe tomorrow I will make scrambled eggs and bacon.*

Deep down inside Faith knew she wouldn't make anything except a b-line to the fridge for a beer or two. *What? No. I am not drinking tomorrow morning. Today I just lost control, but tomorrow I will have control. Besides I will just drink everything tonight so that there won't be anything in the fridge.* Confident in her plan, Faith went off to yank her son out of bed.

Standing in his doorway, a furious rage welled up from deep inside her as she saw him still asleep. No uniform on. No shoes on. Backpack flung open with books and papers strung about the room. How could he do this to her again? Didn't he hear her telling them to wake up?

"Damn it! Michael! Wake the hell up! We are going to be late!"

She grabbed his ankles and pulled him out of the bed only careful to avoid his head hitting the nightstand.

"Mom!"

Athena stood behind Faith. "What! How the hell else am I supposed to get him out of bed? We are running late."

"Why are you fucking yelling? I'm trying to sleep here. It's too damn early for your crap." Faith's husband, Matt, hated it when she started the day yelling at the kids which seemed to be a habit of hers lately.

Matt yelled from his room. More wrath oozed forth from within. *I should have had two beers. No matter. I'm getting drunk tonight. If this is how my day is going to go, I will need to drink.*

"Your son won't get out of bed, so I helped. Unlike some people I have to be at work early in the morning!"

Her husband shouted from his room, not to help, but to find a way to silence the mad dog barking orders at everyone.

"Michael! Get up and get ready for school! Do what your mother says."

Finally, the young boy grew tired of the shouting, the cursing. "Alright! I'm up, God."

Faith glared at Michael. "Don't say God like that and don't shout at me."

Wiping the sleep from his eyes, Michael blankly blinked at her unable to understand how his mother who just cussed him into a state of wakefulness after yanking him out of bed, could be butthurt over his tone. "Whatever."

Faith stood in the foyer, her own backpack over her shoulder urgently tapping her foot and constantly checking her phone. Athena and Mary, stood close by unwilling to tempt the tyrant further. "Michael! Let's go!"

Her husband shouted back. "Stop yelling. Is that all you can do?"

Disgust. Indignation. Faith was not able to keep calm. "Oh, shut the hell up and go back to sleep."

Michael walked into the foyer clothes wrinkled and barely put together. Faith saw the mess of a son in front of her, but couldn't be bothered to care in that moment. All that mattered then and there was getting them to school on time and in one piece. "Let's go."

The tiny family in a giant tornado pulled into the private school parking lot—corner store donuts in hand. A certain relief mixed with a certain dread filled Faith as she cut off the SUV's engine. "We made it."

Her children gathered their bags. Faith's hand shook and tears pooled in her eyes as she watched her three beautiful children put together a morning she had abruptly and angrily brought into fruition. "I'm sorry for yelling. Y'all have a good day. I love you."

Mary scurried into the building. "Love you too, Mom." The

other two just walked away from her in silence all too familiar with the empty apology.

Faith walked up the cement stairs to her classroom. *I can't wait to drink tonight. I need to go by the store to pick up a bottle of red wine and a six pack. I can make it till after work.*

"Good morning Mrs. Smith. How are you?"

I had a beer this morning. Not sure what that means, but it can't be good. My kids hate me. My husband thinks I'm a raving lunatic, which I may be now that I'm thinking about it, I am planning my drinking for tonight, oh and I really don't want to be here talking to you, but other than all of that I'm just peachy. Thanks for asking.

"I'm fine, Mrs. Lopez. How are you?"

"Good. You ready for the meeting today?"

"Crap, I had forgotten about that. It's right after school?"

"Yeah. I hope it doesn't go long, but you know how these meetings can go."

Yes, I do. Somebody always has to ask a stupid question, or add their two cents that no one cares about. "Yes, I do know, but I'm sure it will be a productive meeting. Have a good day."

Mrs. Lopez smiled as she walked down the stairs. "You too. You look like you could use a good day."

What the hell is that supposed to mean? What, do I look like crap or what? Faith opened her classroom door and turned on the lights. She paused for a minute looking out the old giant windows that were the only form of air-conditioning back when the school first opened. The rows of desks were neatly arranged and waiting for the students. An old black chalkboard hung on the east facing wall. A large whiteboard hung on the southern wall. No matter what Faith did she could never get it back to its original white. She spent many lessons decorating that board with information that her students willingly ate up. Faith sat her backpack on the oversized wooden desk that she tried to tuck away in the back corner of the room. She was rarely at the desk.

She preferred to walk around the room to provide one on one instruction.

Faith paused again to gaze out the window. She longed to be outside. It meant freedom. Inside the classroom she felt like a prisoner to a broken way of educating young minds. She felt the overwhelming urge to run. Run where? She had no clue. All she knew standing alone in that room was that she was on the edge of a cliff. She wanted to jump, to fly through the air, to feel a surge of freedom before she smashed into the ground below.

The oversized clock on the wall told her that school was going to start soon and she had once again better step up her pace so she could at least pretend to be on her game. She organized her teacher aides and prayed for God to help her get through the day. The first bell rang. "Here we go."

Faith braced herself to meet her students at the door. They gave her hope in a black hole that was growing larger inside of her with each day. Each academic competition, each athletic event these students stamped their name on the competition's mind. They came from the bottom of the socioeconomic ladder and never stopped fighting to be at the top. Nothing stood in their way.

She stood in the doorway listening to their chatter and giggles. The stress of the morning began to melt away. Despite her disapproval of how education brow beat facts into young minds and left no room for creative thought, she loved teaching. In that act of teaching she lost herself and all of the insanity that tore through her mind. When she was teaching the world around her stopped and it was just her and her students. Faith thrived on seeing a student come into the dawn of understanding. Nothing is more beautiful than seeing someone emerge from the foggy mist of confusion into the light of realization. Teaching brought joy to Faith.

Inside the classroom, few were as good as Faith. She had a

God given ability to shape minds of mush into productive thinking machines. It was outside of the classroom that Faith fell apart.

"Good morning, Mrs. Smith."

"Good morning guys. Your writing prompt is on the board. You know what to do."

The rest of the day went smoothly. The morning had melted into memory. Students completed their assignments. Faith performed her duties as she did every day. Before she realized it, the dismissal bell rang. Students poured out of the building allowing the faculty to drift into the teacher's lounge for the meeting. Faith was one of the first ones in the room. Mrs. Lopez was already there waiting for the meeting to start. She looked up from her phone. "Hello, Mrs. Smith. How was your day?"

Faith sat next to Mrs. Lopez. "It went pretty good. You?"

"Can't complain. Hey, have you finished entering those essays to the archdiocese?"

Groaning inside, Faith pulled out her phone to check her messages. "No, I haven't. I'm almost done."

"You do realize that they are due by the end of the week which is tomorrow? You've had two months to do them."

Faith open and closed her fists as she looked at Mrs. Lopez. "Yes, I do. I will get it done tonight."

"Good. You know how competitive the principal is. She wants our students to win this contest."

"I'm well aware of how the principal is. Like I said, it will be done tonight."

Mrs. Lopez went to speak again when the principal walked in to start the meeting. Faith was glad that the conversation with Mrs. Lopez was over. She hated being reminded of all the work she had to get done outside of the classroom. Truth was she was behind on getting those essays entered just as she was behind on grading and organizing the upcoming academic competition her students were participating in. *I need a damn drink. Let's get this meeting started so we can end it and I can get home. First stop, the store for some mommy juice.*

The principal opened the meeting with a prayer and words of encouragement for the faculty. "I appreciate everyone's hard work this week. We have worked really well as a team this past year to pull this school back from the brink of closure."

Sanders shuffled some papers that were strewn across the table in front of her. "I want to emphasize, however, that we have to keep putting in the hard work. Mid-spring is the most difficult time of the year because we are tired, the students are tired, and the finish line is visible."

The teachers nodded their heads in agreement. She continued. "Yet, we have to buckle down and finish with a bang. We have several competitions at the elementary and Jr. high levels that we are involved in. I need all teachers to be at their best. Mrs. Smith can you give us an update on the archdiocese essay contest and the Honors Academic Competition?"

A sinking feeling pooled in the pits of Faith's stomach. *I'm going to have to lie my way out of this. Why do I put off everything to the last minute?* "Everything is going well. I will have the essays entered tonight. Having read the essays I feel confident that we will hold our own against the other schools. The Honors Academic Competition (HAC) is going well. I have every confidence that our students will do well."

Principal Sanders smiled. The rest of the faculty applauded Faith. All except Lopez. Lopez's forehead wrinkled as her eyes narrowed in on Faith. Faith merely looked away not wanting to confront whatever was annoying Lopez.

"That's great news Mrs. Smith. Keep me posted on how the students do at the essay contest and arrange to meet with me during your conference period tomorrow so we can discuss the upcoming HAC. If anyone doesn't have anything to add, questions, or comments we can end the meeting and go home."

Faith held her breath. She could feel her hands beginning to shake. *Weird. I wonder why my hands are shaking. I just hope no one asks her any questions. Please no one say anything.*

Silence. *Thank you Jesus. Time to go home.*

Principal Sanders smiled. "Okay everyone. Go home and have a good evening. Tomorrow is Friday!"

Chairs scraped against the white tiled floor. Murmuring filled the room. Faith gathered her stuff and made for the door. "Mrs. Smith."

Crap.

Mrs. Lopez stood behind Faith. "I'm really concerned that you are not going to get those essays in. Are you sure you are going to be able to handle that?"

Annoyed Faith turned around to face her, putting her hands on her hips and biting her tongue. "Yes, I'm sure. Why do you ask? What is the big deal with you about that?"

"You haven't exactly been on your game lately. You're not joining any of the committees. You botched the Christmas fundraiser and I had to cover you. The principal may not have noticed, but I have. I don't know what is going on with you, but are you okay? Do you need any help?"

Help? I don't need any damn help. What's her problem with me?
"No, I don't need any help. I will get those essays done tonight. Thank you for asking. Everything is fine."

"Don't let us down."

Faith walked out of the room to go pick up her kids from the after school program. Her fingernails dug deeply into her palms. *Don't let us down? Who the hell does she think she is? I have always done my damn job and now she is questioning me like I'm some kind of slacker. No matter. I'll get the essays done tonight so she will leave me the hell alone about it.*

"Momma!"

"Hey Mary." Faith reached down to hug her baby. Michael and Athena smiled as they walked to greet her at the door. "Hey guys. How was school today?"

Athena was always the first to answer that question and always with the same answer. "Boring. No tea to spill today."

Faith signaled them out of the room and began walking down the hall to the exit doors. "Oh darn, no gossip to fill me in on? How about you Michael?"

Michael pretended to kick a soccer ball down the hall. "Nothing special. Just a day. How about you?"

The afternoon sun baked into Faith's pale skin. "My day was good. We have to run by the store before we go home."

Athena plopped into the passenger seat. "For what?"

Faith hated that question. "For my stuff."

Athena rolled her eyes. "You mean your wine, beer, and cigarettes. Seriously, does that have to be an everyday thing?"

Faith swallowed her frustration and pulled out of the parking lot. She started the day on a negative note; she wasn't going to end it on that same note. "I drink to take the edge off the day. It's fine."

"Everyday fine?"

"Just drop it. Please."

Faith drove to the store while listening to the kids babble on about what happened that day. They were arguing over who was going to play the PlayStation first at home while they walked into the store. Faith turned and walked down her favorite aisle. She pretended to be searching for the perfect bottle of red wine, but all that really mattered was the price. She got the cheapest she could. It wasn't about the taste anyway. It was always about that effect.

Faith went to the self-check-out line. She always did. She liked the anonymity the line gave her. No pesky cashier to pass a judging glance her way. The beer bottles rattled as she put them into the cart and wheeled them to the car. She loved the sound of those bottles, for soon she would be throwing them back and enjoying her evening in front of the computer getting those damn essays entered.

She checked out of the store and eagerly walked through the parking lot to her car. The ride home seemed long. All she could think about was taking that first drink. She pulled into her driveway anxious to get inside and pour a glass of wine. She earned it. That Lopez was getting on her nerves with all of the questions. "Mom, what's for dinner?"

Michael was bouncing behind her as she unlocked the door. "I don't know. Whatever Dad brings home."

"But that's what you have said every night this week. When are you going to cook again?"

Since Faith started working, dinner was never at the top of her to do list. It was always get through work, get home, and get the drink on. "I do work now. Why am I the only one who has to worry about dinner?"

Athena walked down the hall to her room. "But you're not, Dad is. You don't cook anymore. You aren't ever worried about dinner since you stopped eating dinner. Which is unhealthy by the way. You're not going to get fat just because you eat dinner."

Faith never did eat dinner anymore. She drank instead. She let her family and friends believe she had an eating disorder because it was better than them knowing that the real reason she didn't eat was because it messed up her buzz. She drank her dinner and that's just how it was now. The family would just have to deal with it.

Faith called down the hall. "I'll make sure Dad gets something good."

She walked into the kitchen. Standing there reminded her of this morning. Seemed so long ago and not that big of a deal.

That one beer was nothing. She was still able to do her job and the best part of it was that no one knew. She wasn't going to do it again. Only alcoholics drank every morning and she was not an alcoholic. Faith found the corkscrew and opened the wine. She loved the sound of the cork popping out of the bottle. It was a delightful sound. She poured the wine into the crystal glass she had inherited from her grandmother.

Faith held her nose over the glass briefly to inhale that sweet smell that only red wine could offer. Then she tipped the warm liquid into her mouth. Instant gratification reigned down her throat and up into her brain. *Finally, I can relax.*

Without further hesitation, Faith got her computer out and began entering those essays. If she was going to thoroughly enjoy her drinking, she was going to have to get those essays out of the way.

A couple of hours and glasses of wine later, Faith was done with the essays. Sometime in that duration her husband had come home and fed the kids. She had barely taken notice. He was gone again to soccer practice with Michael, so Faith was free to drink without hovering eyes. Or, so she thought. "Mom?"

Faith looked over at Athena who was watching her with concern. "Yes, honey?"

"I don't suppose you can take me to the corner store to get some ice cream?"

A twinge of guilt flickered in Faith. "You would suppose correctly. Why didn't you ask me sooner? I'll text your dad to pick you up some on his way home."

"Okay." Athena walked away from her mom disappointed and unsure what to think of the woman sitting in front of the T.V guzzling beers after she had already had wine. One thing Athena always knew about her mom was that one was never enough.

Faith threw away her beer and decided to finish off the bottle of wine before drinking another beer. She took her wine outside and sat under the huge oak tree that branched over the whole backyard. Puffing on her cigarette, Faith looked up at the night sky. A realization dawned on her with a sudden force. *I'm a drunk. I'm always going to be a drunk. I will die with a drink in my hand and I'm okay with that. It's just who I am.*

THE MORNING COFFEE shop rush had subsided. Faith's cup was empty. An empty coffee cup was a crisis in her world and would not be tolerated for long. "I need another cup."

Carol glanced at Faith's oversized cup that technically held two cups of coffee rather than the standard one cup. Faith grinned. "I've always been one to overindulge. These days it's coffee. Love me some good old fashioned coffee."

Carol smirked. "I can see that. I've never been one for coffee."

"Now, that is a foreign concept to me. What is life without coffee? How do you even get out of bed without that delicious smell of coffee brewing in the house? How does one communicate with other humans without that wonderful first cup? No one dares talk to me before all of my senses have enjoyed the coffee till it's gone."

"It's possible. I promise."

"Pfft. Not in my world. I'll be right back." Faith stood to walk to the counter for another cup, or two, of heaven's tonic. She looked over her shoulder to take notice of Carol.

Carol's head hung low. Her chin almost touched her chest. Slowly, she brought her hand to her lips. She began to chew her nails as her hair fell around her face. Faith wondered if she was trying to hide.

Interesting. I wonder if I looked as broken as she does when I first sobered up. Sad really that we all have to be in great pain before we can pull ourselves out of the misery that plagues us. Rare is the human who journeys through life without enduring the bouts of mental anguish that inspire spiritual change. Some of us have to go down into the dark depths of hell before we elect ourselves worthy of actually being happy. The process of dying to the old self is painful. Getting rid of old habits and ways of thinking is much like a child trying to discard their favorite blanket.

Faith returned baring two cups of coffee. "Here, I bought you a cup. Here is the cream and sugar. If you don't like it no worries, but I can't sit here and drink alone. Did enough of that over the years."

Carol took the cup. "Thank you. I'll give it a try."

"I saw you watching me watching you. I can see your mind working overtime. What are you thinking?"

Carol sipped her coffee and frowned. "I have some questions. Why did you hit yourself? What was happening to you? When you drank that morning did you know you were an alcoholic?"

Laughter erupted from Faith. "I wish I could tell you with perfect clarity what was going on in my mind, but I was in the throws of addiction and mental illness. Many times I stood on the edge of a cliff screaming into the wind for someone to help me, but no one heard me. I was just dramatic, as Matt always said. I was just a kid. I was just not spiritual enough. I was just this or just that, but there's one thing I knew I wasn't, and that was normal. Deep down I knew the wires in my mind were crossed and tangled into a knot that hijacked hope and joy."

Faith's coffee shop companion furrowed her eyebrows. "And did you know that you were an alcoholic? You didn't answer my question."

Waving her finger, Faith smiled. "You caught me. I don't like to admit it, but to answer your question, no. No, I still had some experimenting to do before I would admit that I was an alcoholic. I mean I had questioned whether or not I was one, but I had always reached the conclusion that since I had a job, a house, and a family that I was good. What I failed to see at that point was that everything was holding on by a thread."

Carol nodded. "It's hard."

"What? To look at your reflection and not know who the hell you are let alone what the hell you are doing?"

"Exactly."

"You have to break through some molds, most of which are your own creation, before you can take those first few steps toward sanity. But first you have to realize that you are in control of jack shit."

Carol huffed. "What is sanity? I don't think I know anymore."

"If you are anything like I was, you haven't known sanity in a long time." Faith pushed her hand through her hair. "You have been too busy dancing to the demons' song to remember, if you ever even knew, sanity. Sanity comes in different forms, but the commonality of all types is that you know peace of mind. You are free."

Putting down her coffee, Carol plopped her back into the seat. "Free? I am free?"

"Sure, you are. That's why you do anything for that next drink, that next high. Yeah that's freedom. Truth is most of humanity is a slave in one form, or another."

"If you say so. So, when did you know that you were an alcoholic?"

Faith paused for several moments. "That's not such an easy answer. Deep down I knew for several years. When I couldn't even go one day without a drink, I think I knew. However, one weekend I found myself absolutely lost in the drink. Reality completely abandoned me. I knew I needed help then, but I didn't actually believe I was an alcoholic until I had several months sobriety, but that is a story for later."

Carol grimaced as she took another sip of coffee. "So, when did you get help."

"When my sanity, my whole world started slipping through my fingers."

TROUBLED WATERS

*D*id you get those essays entered? You've had two months to deal with them."

Enough with the damn essays already. "Yes, I did. I finished them last night."

Mrs. Lopez popped her biscuit in the teacher lounge's microwave. "About time. You had me worried."

Faith put the hazelnut cream in her coffee. Her face tightened. "I told you I would get it done and I did."

Standing in front of the microwave Mrs. Lopez put her hand on her hip. "You don't have to be so grouchy about it."

Faith's stomach burned and churned deep inside of her. Months of silently enduring Mrs. Lopez's constant watchful eye and underhanded comments were taking their toll. Faith had had enough. She wanted to tell her off. To tell her what she really thought of all her crap. The only thing holding her tongue was their former friendship. Once upon a time they had been what some would call best friends, but lately that had changed. Faith wasn't sure why, but she was sure she was done with the condescending witch standing in front of her. "Maybe I don't appreciate you constantly checking up on my work. When I say I'm going to do something, I get it done."

The microwave dinged. Mrs. Lopez stood frozen glaring back at Faith. "Maybe if you weren't half-assing your work, I wouldn't have to check up on you."

Faith stepped forward. "Half-assing my work! Wow, just, wow."

Lopez shifted back and forth on her feet. "I don't know what's going on with you, but you have not been pulling your weight around here. Which means I have to pull double duty to cover your ass!"

Faith rolled her eyes. "Oh, here we go."

Faith shuffled back and forth on her feet shifting her body a little closer to Lopez. "I forgot you are the poor martyr who is the only one who does anything around here. I completely forgot that only you have problems. Only you help the principal. You are the only one who cares about the kids. Of course! It's always about you. What do you think should be happening? How do you think people should be acting?"

Faith slapped her forehead with her palm. "How stupid of me. I need to be more like you. That's what you want right? For everyone to do, to say, and to act the way you think they should. God help anyone going through anything."

Lopez's mouth hung open unable to speak. Finally, she half whispered. "Where is all of this coming from? If you are so angry at me then tell me what you are going through! Help me to understand! What is going on?"

Violently shaking her head, Faith spoke through a clenched jaw. "No! You don't get to do that. You don't get to pretend to care. Do me a favor and leave me alone. I will get the job done. Maybe not the way you want it done, but we can't all be like you!"

Faith grabbed her coffee with shaking hands and left Mrs. Lopez frozen in a shocked stance by the microwave. She didn't move. She didn't speak. She just stood with her mouth hanging open.

Walking down the hallway, Faith couldn't believe what she had said. *What have I done? Why did I yell at her? She is probably going to run to Sanders and tell on me. Whatever. I don't need this job. I don't need this place. I don't need these people. I'm so done with this place.*

"Mrs. Smith? Are you okay?" One of her students looked up at her concern written all over her face.

Faith mustered the biggest smile she could. "I'm fine, honey. I'm just fine."

The student's eyes grew big. Something behind Faith had caught her attention. She was looking over Faith's shoulders when she said, "Good morning, Mrs. Sanders."

"Good morning." Mrs. Sanders looked towards Faith. "Don't forget to come by my office during your off period. I want to talk about the HAC."

Dread filled Faith. She hadn't prepared anything for the competition and was unsure how she was going to B.S. her way through the meeting. Why had she put it off for so long? She couldn't wait for this day to just be over. *I'm getting wasted tonight.* "Yes, Ma'am."

The morning dragged on with Faith obsessing over what to say about the HAC. She gave the students busy work allowing her to work on her computer, so she could attempt to pull something together that didn't sound like she did it last minute. She planned on working through lunch when Mrs. Lopez entered her room. "Hey, can we talk?"

Faith peered over her computer to see Lopez's dark brown eyes glistening with tears. "Sure."

Lopez pulled a chair in front of Faith's desk. "I've been thinking about what you said and I think we should talk about it. I think we both have a lot on our minds and it would be better if we talked our way through it."

Faith's hands began to shake while her stomach began to flip inside of her. "I shouldn't have yelled at you."

Faith leaned back in her chair. "For that I am sorry. I'm just under a lot of pressure here and at home."

Lopez leaned forward. "What's going on at home that is leaking here?

Moments of silence hung in the air. Lopez pressed further. "Honestly you have been MIA for several months. You aren't as active in the school as you once were. It's like you are pulling away and I don't know why."

A small voice inside begged Faith to come clean to Lopez, to tell her about the drinking that was taking hold of her life, but the louder voice told her to be quiet because no one would understand. "I don't really want to talk about it, but I will try to work harder here. It isn't fair to you or the principal for me to not be at my best."

Lopez watched Faith. "Are you sure you don't want to talk about it?"

She placed her hand on Faith's. "We don't get through this life alone that is why God gave us community. In the community we help each other during difficult times."

Faith shook her head and slid her hand out from under Lopez. "Yes, I'm sure and thank you for saying that about the whole community thing. That means a lot to me."

Lopez moved to leave the room. "See you at lunch?"

"Not today. I have to finish up some things."

Lopez left Faith to sit in her classroom with no one but herself to blame for the upcoming mess of a meeting she had to get through. *Maybe I should just tell her I put if off to the last minute. No, I can't. Maybe I could tell her that I have been sick. No, she isn't going to believe that. Shit! She is going to be so damn mad at me. Crap, what am I going to do? I could really use a drink right now.*

Another period came after lunch and went rapidly pushing Faith to meet Sanders face to face. Faith looked at the speeding clock on the wall. The hands of time were telling her that now was the moment for Faith to confront Sanders. The hour had come to look her in the eyes and disappoint one of the few people Faith respected. Slowly, Faith made her way down the stairs and through the white walled long narrow hallway that led to the office. Each step struck a sense of panic into Faith. She knocked on Sanders' door. An authoritative voice answered back, "Come in."

Faith swallowed the fear that had begun to choke her and entered the small office. Sanders sat behind a large brown wooden desk that held two computers, a calendar, and several files. She gestured for Faith to take a seat in one of the large grey lounge chairs that had always welcomed her before, but now felt more like an electric chair. Watching Faith, Sanders pushed her laptop to the side. "So, where are you on HAC?"

Faith hesitated. *What am I supposed to say? The truth? I can't tell her that I just didn't do it. How did I even get to this point? Crap. What am I going to tell her?*

Sanders leaned forward on her hands that were resting on her desk. Her finger gently slid across her bottom lip as she studied Faith. "You haven't done anything on HAC have you?"

And there it is. The truth. Funny how that little bastard seems to squirm out no matter how hard you try to hide it. I just have to tell her the truth. God, I'm going to lose my job. I should lose my job. I failed at getting this competition dealt with.

Faith could no longer look her boss in the eyes. She stared at her fingers interlocking each other. "No, no I haven't."

Sanders' expression fell into anger. Her eyes grew smaller and furiously focused on Faith. The once invisible fine lines began to span across her forehead as she scowled. The once beautiful woman put on the mask of fury. Seconds, that felt like minutes, passed between the two of them before Sanders spoke. "Why?"

How am I supposed to answer that when I don't even know why I didn't do it?

Oh, come on. You know exactly why you failed.

No, I don't. I just kept putting it off and putting it off till now. I was busy and tired. I have a lot going on right now I can't be asked to always do more. I mean I do have a life outside of this school for God sakes.

Seriously? You were drunk. It's that simple.

No. It's not that. I was just really busy and this project slipped away from me.

You were drunk.

I wish I was drunk now.

Faith couldn't look up. "I don't know. Time just slipped away from me."

"That's no excuse. We are all busy and have families. You let us all down. This isn't the first time you have failed at maintaining your responsibilities. Remember the Christmas Fundraiser?"

Does she really have to bring that up again. I was sick for crying out loud.

You were hungover. Sick, hungover it's all the same. "I remember."

Sanders leaned back into her brown leather chair. "You were supposed to help organize, set up, and serve. You did none of it and your responsibilities fell upon Mrs. Lopez to carry out. As it will again. I'm taking HAC away from you and handing it over to Lopez. I don't know what is going on with you, but I suggest that you get your act together. Next time you fail me I'm writing you up. There better not be a next time."

Shame collapsed over the pride Faith once had in her work. Her shoulders slumped over. Her head hung down. Her chin gently kissed her chest. She couldn't bring her eyes up to meet Sanders. Instead she watched her fingers pull at her nails. "I understand. It won't happen again."

"I suggest you apologize to Lopez for making this her problem."

"Of course."

"Go. Leave before I change my mind and write you up for this infraction. Smith?"

Faith stood to leave. "Yes?"

"Whatever is going on, I'm here to help. I'm always here to talk to. I care about you."

Tears burned Faith's eyes. She wanted to tell her that she was drowning and didn't know how to swim anymore. She wanted to beg her for help, but she wasn't sure what to tell her. She wasn't sure what was going on with her. All she knew for certain was that her world was collapsing around her and she didn't know how to fix any of it. "Thank you. I appreciate that."

Faith left the office and climbed the mountain of stairs back to her classroom. One more class to go and she could go home and hide, but first she was going to have to confront Lopez. *The absolute last person I want to talk to is the one person I must talk to. I can't believe I let her down too. I let everyone down. I'm a piece of crap. No wonder Lopez wants little to do with me.*

Faith's hands were shaking as she readied the papers for her students to complete. Her stomach was twisted into burning knots that seem to ripple with nausea every time she moved. *Just one more hour to go and I'm free. One. More. Hour.*

The dismissal bell rang. Kids scurried to their lockers laughing and joking eager for the weekend. Faith gathered up her stuff and her courage. It was time to confront Lopez. They both had auditorium duty, so at least Faith didn't have to hunt her down.

Faith entered the noisy auditorium where the kids all gathered to wait for parents to pick them up. Lopez was standing in the middle as she always did to talk with the students. Lopez looked up and saw Faith. No smile. No wave. She already knew.

Might as well get this over with. Faith gradually made her way to talk with Lopez. Every step felt like a ton of lead weighted down each leg. Lopez's eyes never left Faith's. "I need to talk to you for a minute."

Lopez stood still. "I already know what you are going to say. Sanders gave me the HAC because you didn't get it done. Now I have to spend all weekend fixing your screwup. I told you to ask for help if you needed it. I would have been more than happy to help, but now I have to do all of it."

Stuttering Faith moved to speak. "I can help you with..."

Lopez waved her hand. "No, Sanders doesn't want you anywhere near it. I don't want you anywhere near it. You messed up."

Guilt began to rush over Faith. As she did with Sanders, she hung her head unable to make eye contact. "I'm sorry. I didn't mean for this to happen."

Lopez rolled her eyes then looked down at Faith. She shook her head. "You never do. Lately, you are not the same person you were last year. You need to get your life together." Lopez walked away from Faith leaving her to drown in her own guilt and remorse.

Faith stood in a room full of people alone. Forever alone. "Mom?" Athena stood in front of Faith concern written all over her face. "Are you okay? Did you and Lopez have a fight?"

Faith wanted to cry, to confess everything, but what would she confess? How could she explain what was going on when she didn't know. She suspected that alcohol was a major problem, but she really didn't know. She lied, "It's okay baby. Lopez and I are fine. You ready to go?"

Athena straightened herself, making her appear taller, more defiant. "I don't believe you. Nobody does. Not Dad, not Lopez, not any of your students. You say you are fine, but we can see you. You never smile a real smile anymore. Your eyes are different. Like something is missing. Something is wrong. Why won't you tell us? Why won't you let us help you?"

She didn't know what to say. What do you say to your child who is begging you to tell the truth? *Do you dare tell a soul so young that it's untarnished that your own soul is turning black and you have no idea how to stop it?* "There is nothing to tell. Get your stuff and let's go."

Athena snatched up her backpack frustrated at the blatant lie and walked toward the car. Michael and Mary followed behind her talking all about their day. Athena abruptly stopped and turned to face her mom. Her eyes were wide and dark. Her lips turned down. "You're lying. You preach at us that lying is a sin, but you are looking me in my face and lying. You're selfish and I don't know who you are."

Athena's words pierced Faith's heart. Just as she did with Sanders and Lopez, Faith hung her head low. The weight of her shame was to much to carry. She followed her kids to the car listening to Mary and Michael. They knew their mom was not well, but desperately hung onto the thread of hope that everything would magically turn out fine. Faith didn't hear their conversation. She occasionally mumbled a response when prompted, but her mind was caught in the memory of today.

Like she did every day, Faith pulled into her driveway. Except today she felt hopeless, confused. Faith walked into the house, sat down in her chair, and waited. She just sat and listened to the kids fight over snacks. No TV. No phone. She just sat and stared at the blank television screen wishing that she was somewhere far far away. She didn't know how much time had passed, but she heard her husband walk in the house. Mary hollered, "Daddy!"

His deep voice answered back. "Hey baby. Where is your mom?"

Mary swung her legs back and forth at the breakfast table while she played her computer game. Without looking up from her computer, she answered her dad. "Sitting in her chair. She has been sitting there a long time."

Faith continued to sit in her chair without moving. She heard Mary's response. *Great. Now he is going to ask me what is wrong and, once again, I won't be able to answer. If I knew what was wrong I would fix it.*

Matt walked over to Faith. "What's wrong with you?"

He stood before her waiting for her to respond. Faith kept her eyes cast down. She couldn't look him in the eyes. She let another lie pass from her lips. "Nothing. Just a long day."

Matt rolled his eyes. "Yeah, well so was mine. What are we doing for dinner?"

Sudden fury overcame Faith. Her fists tightened. Her jaw clenched. She was tired of people wanting something from her all of the time. She gave and she gave and it was never enough. "How the hell should I know!"

Shock that grew into anger flooded his eyes. "What the hell is your problem? What, you want me to figure out dinner just like I have done every night this damn week?"

Her inner demon frolicked. It was ready to unleash upon Matt. Faith made eye contact with Matt for the first time since he had gotten home. Her eyes bore into him. "I don't give a shit what we eat. You're the one who is hungry, you figure it out."

He leaned over her trapping her in the chair. "Don't you talk to me that way you bitch. You have kids to feed, or have you forgotten that?"

That was all she needed. Him calling her a bitch was the last chain to unlock the demon that craved to be unleashed. She lifted her chin and lowered her voice to a near growl. "Go fuck yourself and get the hell away from me! I take care of those kids everyday as I have for years while you sit around and do nothing."

He leaned in even closer—his breath hot on her cheeks. "You are crazy. You know that? You have always been crazy. I'm taking the kids to get something to eat. You just sit here and be the crazy bitch you are."

"I'm crazy? Listen here you son of a bitch, I have carried this family through thick and thin while you sat around and did nothing, but barely work at that piece-a-shit job you have that couldn't pay our bills to save our lives."

He clenched his fists. Wrath swallowed him. "I work my ass off for this family while you sit around and drink every night. You used to be a strong woman of faith and now you are a fucking drunk! I should divorce you."

Hysterical laughter rocked Faith. "Please do! I would love a divorce. Give me the papers and I will sign them gladly!"

"Stop it! Just stop it!" Athena cried out from her petite frame. Her dark eyes filled with tears as she held onto the crying Mary. "Why do you guys have to say those ugly things to each other?"

Guilt swept over Faith as she looked at her crying daughters knowing that once again her actions had caused more pain and suffering. *Just like earlier. I'm a piece of crap. What kinda mother makes her kids cry?*

He snapped back at the girls. "It's your mother! Talk to her. She is the crazy one."

Athena glared at her father. "You're both crazy."

He moved to argue with Athena. Faith stood up. "Just stop. Let it go. Y'all go get dinner."

Matt's black stormy eyes scanned Faith up and down. "And just what the hell are you going to do while we are gone. Drink?"

Faith argued with the demon within who begged to verbally tear Matt apart. She spoke through gritted teeth. "Why can't you ever just shut up? You just go on and on and on. Go to dinner and leave me the hell alone."

He began to stomp away from her. "Whatever, but I'm not getting your shit!"

Faith grinned. "Don't need you too. I took care of all that myself. I didn't want to listen to you bitch."

He stood in front of her swaying back and forth as he did when he argued. He wanted to say more, but Athena stopped him. "Let's just go, please."

"Come on kids. Let's leave your mother alone. That seems to be what she wants these days."

Faith stood in the kitchen staring at the wine bottle while listening to her family leave the house. *Finally.*

She popped open the wine bottle savoring that sweat smell. Quickly she poured the wine into the glass. She thought about just drinking straight from the bottle, but only alcoholics do that, so she drank from the glass.

Faith went to sit in her dark blue chair and turned the T.V. on to some reality show that held no meaning, no content just the way Faith wanted her life.

Drop, drop, dropping into the void. Nothing mattered here. Here in the great in-between all of life's worries slipped away. Faith closed her eyes. She could feel the slight spin of the room. Not too fast; not too slow. Just right like a slowing down merry-go-round. She could feel her limbs tingling tenderly to the tips. Blessed nothingness wrapped in a blanket of welcoming sensations that lifted the psyche into a different dimension engulfed her. Here she was safe. Here she was loved.

Faith had heard her family come home. Heard them talk to her. Heard them leave her in her chair.

"Mom? Mom?"

The voice broke through the haze. Athena stood over Faith.

"What do you want?"

Uneasy, Athena answered. "I was wondering if you could help me with my homework."

Opening her eyes Faith looked into a child's eyes that looked back at her with fear. She wanted to comfort her, to help her, but the void pulled her back into its embrace leaving her to say what had become her mantra. "Go ask your dad."

Athena hung her head to hide the tears in her eyes and walked away to leave her mother drifting in the void.

Trip, trip, tripping into the spinning nothingness of the mind. Time has no meaning. Pain has no hold. People come in and people drift away. Memory is nothing more than a hazy horizon in the rear view mirror.

Breathe in. Breathe out. Heartbeat thumps to an unknown rhythm. Bodies sink into the chair around her. What is here or there matters no more.

Faith's eyes fluttered open. The green digital clock on the cable box read 12:36 a.m. A half empty beer stood next to her inviting her to finish the warm sour liquid. She reached out to grab the beer.

She knew she was dying. Her soul screamed for her to stop, but the body hollered "More!"

Faith sat up and drank the beer. She fumbled out of the chair. She heard the TV playing in the other room which meant that Matt was still up. She didn't want to see him, hear him or deal with any crap he might throw at her.

She crept into the kitchen to get another beer and a cigarette. "Still drinking?"

He stood in the doorway leading into the dining room. Faith

couldn't give less of a crap about what he thought. She didn't want to fight, but the demon was rattling at its unlocked cage. "It's my last one."

He stepped closer to her as she pulled the beer out of the fridge. "I don't want to fight with you."

Annoyed Faith opened the beer and chugged. "I'm not fighting. I'm just going to smoke this and then go to bed."

"I didn't mean what I said about divorce."

Unable to stop herself Faith responded. "I did. I want a divorce."

Pain tore through his soul. "You don't mean that. You're just drunk."

"Okay, whatever you say." Faith stumbled outside with Matt behind her.

"I think we should talk about this."

"I don't. There is nothing to talk about."

"What happened today that got you so mad?"

Faith puffed on her cigarette. "Nothing, it was just a long day." She put out her cigarette. "I'm going to bed."

Matt followed her through the house and to the bedroom. "Something happened. Why else would you want to fight with me today?"

"I didn't want to fight with you. You came in the house with an attitude. You came in looking for a fight. You always come at me looking for a fight. I was just sitting there minding my own business." Faith pulled down the covers on her king sized bed hoping that it would signal to Matt that she did not want to talk anymore about anything with him.

Matt crossed his arms. A fire lit in his eyes. Faith knew that fire; knew that it would ignite a storm that would wreak havoc. "I just came home to find my wife sitting and staring at nothing for god knows how long. I was trying to get you to snap out of it.

You're not yourself. I'm trying to find you, but you won't let me. Why won't you let me help you?"

Faith laid down relishing the soft touch of her pillow. Her eyes grew heavy. The void she loved so much was calling back to her willing to hold her forever in its embrace. "By yelling at me? Yeah you snapped me out of it alright. Your answer to everything is to yell."

"And your answer to everything is to fight. You know how you are when you get in those moods. You need someone to slap some sense into you."

"Whatever. I just want to go to sleep. Leave me alone."

Matt uncrossed his arms and reached out to stroke her hair. "Do you still want the divorce?"

Faith's eyes closed. Her words were barely audible. The embrace of the void was tightening. "I just want to sleep. Let me sleep."

With that Faith drifted into the world of dreamless sleep happy to feel nothing but the dark.

Sunlight broke across Faith's eyes forcing her to open them up to a world filled with misery. Last night's void was today's hell. She wanted to hide from everyone, but life carries on whether you are on board for the ride or not. She got out of bed. Walking through the house she realized no one was awake yet. As usual she went to make coffee and once again there was beer in the fridge. This time there were several beers left over. This time it was a Saturday morning. No work. No students to smell her breath. No one was awake. No one needed to know. *Screw it.*

Faith popped open a beer and chugged it down as fast as she could bare the burning in her throat. *What the hell am I doing? Stop, put the beer down. Just stop. You don't need this.*

Faith reached for the second beer. *Screw it. It's the weekend. Lots of people drink in the morning and all day on the weekends. You had a rough week you earned this.*

But this isn't right.

What's wrong about it? You aren't breaking any laws. You aren't hurting anyone. Just enjoy it. Besides, who is going to know? Everyone is still asleep. Drink your precious coffee afterwards and the only thing anyone will smell is coffee and stale cigarettes. Down the hatch!

Faith popped open the second beer. *This is my last one this morning. I'll drink again later.*

She stood outside smoking a cigarette unable to believe that she just downed two beers before noon on a Saturday.

"Mommy? I'm hungry."

Faith jumped out of her skin. "Crap! You scared me."

Mary laughed. "Sorry, I thought you saw me."

"Nope, guess I was lost in my own head. I will make some scrambled eggs and bacon. Okay?"

Mary jumped up and down. "Yes! Eggs and bacon. I love bacon. It's a gift from heaven." Mary turned to yell at Michael! "Mom is going to make some bacon."

Faith put out her cigarette and went into the kitchen to cook the breakfast. Michael came barreling around the corner of the kitchen counter. "Bacon! Where is it!"

Faith smiled. "I haven't started cooking it yet."

"Hurry, Mom. I'm starving."

"Starving huh?"

"Yes."

"What's all the noise about?" Matt walked into the kitchen half asleep. "Did I hear something about bacon?"

Michael pretended to kick a soccer ball. "Mom is making bacon."

Mary twirled over the tile floor. "Bacon, bacon, bacon!"

Laughing Faith starting cooking the bacon. "What's on the agenda today?"

Matt poured a cup of coffee. "Don't you remember? My dad is having a BBQ at his house at 1. Everyone is going to be there."

"Oh, yeah. Sounds like fun."

Breakfast was served to chattering children. Faith relished in the small moments that she overlooked during the chaos of the work week. *Know what you need? A drink. That small buzz is slipping away. Go get another beer.*

Faith sat frozen in her chair half listening to her children talk about their favorite anime shows. *Where did that come from? I'm not drinking now. I'll wait till the party. I can wait till the party then it's on. I'm going to get messed up, but not too messed up.*

Faith began clearing the table. She looked at her kids. "Time to get ready to go. Brush your teeth and make sure your clothes match."

A couple of hours later the family was at the BBQ. Faith went straight for the cold beer. She had every intention to get buzzed then stop drinking. *Just enough to get buzzed and that's it.*

Time ticked, ticked, ticked on and the drinks kept coming. Faith was lost in the buzz. She knew she should stop and eat something, but she didn't want to let go of that buzz. So, the more the drinks came the more she drank unable to stop. One of Matt's cousins sat down next to her. *Damn. I can't stand this woman. What the hell does she want?*

Slurring her words, the woman leaned over to Faith. "What's up?"

Faith remembered all that this woman had done over the years. She had never liked Faith and had spread rumors about her several times. Whenever she talked lies spewed out. She wanted to tell her to screw off, but managed a decent response. "Not much. What's up with you?"

"I just wanted to let you know that I don't like you very much."

Shocked, Faith sat up in her chair. She had never liked the woman, but had kept the peace through the years. Today, however, Faith had no intention of keeping the peace. "Truth be told, I don't like you either."

No one noticed the two women on the verge of a fight. Matt stood with his father at the BBQ pit several feet away. The children were running around with a soccer ball. Red hibiscus flowers blew in the breeze. Smoke from the pit swirled around the big yard that held fruit trees and a small patch of tomato plants. To the outside observer the yard was a picture perfect day for a family gathering.

The cousin put her beer down on the table. "So, whatcha going to do about it?"

The demon rattling within Faith tasted blood and demanded to go for the kill. Afterall, the bitch deserved it for all the crap she had been talking about Faith for years. Now was the time to deal with this bitch and put her in her place. "I ain't going to do shit about it unless you keep talking your shit."

The cousin leapt up and opened her arms inviting Faith to hit her. "Come on then, bitch. Come get you some."

Slowly, methodically, Faith put her beer down, stood up, and put her face into the face of the drunk woman. "I will fuck you up. Make no mistake I will tear that fat ass up and not think twice about it when I'm done with you."

"Faith! Stop!" Matt called out from across the backyard they were sitting in. Faith knew he had noticed the fight when Faith stood up because his eyes were wide and focused on Faith.

But, Faith couldn't hear him. Her demon was loose and would not stop until the bitch was on the ground where she deserved to be. Faith balled her fist and launched it into the fat face of the cousin who had spent so many years dogging Faith to anyone who would listen. Screaming from kids echoed throughout the yard, but Faith could hear none of it. Down came her fist on the woman's face over and over again. She heard pleas to stop, but the demon was loose. Hands grabbed at her. She shoved them off and pounded the woman again. Arms wrapped around her waist. She kicked at the woman bleeding on the ground.

"Faith! Stop!"

Faith flayed her arms and yanked at Matt's arms. "Let me go! I want to fuck her up!"

Matt got in her face. "Stop it! Just stop it! You need to calm down before they call the police! Faith!"

Heart pounding. Fists pulsating. Breathing heavy. Faith looked into Matt's eyes. "Get me the hell out of here."

"Kids lets go." Matt rushed to gather their stuff while Faith stood ready to lunge at the woman again.

She walked over to the cousin and knelt down to whisper in her ear. "I'm not to be fucked with, bitch. Remember that the next time you want to run your mouth. Remember that the next time you think you have the balls to play with me."

"Faith! Let's go." Matt grabbed Faith's arm and pulled her toward the car that waited in the front driveway.

"Mom, what is wrong with you!" Tears fell from Athena's eyes. "You almost killed her!"

Mary and Michael silently sobbed as they got into the car. Faith didn't care. All she wanted was to finish the woman off. "She deserved what she got for all the crap she said about me. She started it and I finished it."

Pulling out of the driveway, Matt yelled. "What the hell were you thinking!"

Faith looked over at him with hate in her eyes. "I wanted her dead. Maybe if you had defended me against all of her bullshit instead of always telling me to get over it and to shut up, this wouldn't have happened."

"Are you for real right now? You are blaming this on me?"

"If the shoe fits, fucking wear it. You never defend me. In

fact, you always tear me down and you do it in front of everyone."

"Maybe that's 'cause you are fucking crazy."

"Ah, there you go again! Call me crazy one more time and I'll show you crazy." Faith went to slap him across the face she had grown to despise over the years.

He violently grabbed her arm that was about to unleash fury upon his face. Athena screamed. Mary cried. Michael's small hands helped his father grab her arm. Surprising strength held her arm back. Matt squeezed her arm. "I should have let them call the police on you!"

"Mom! Please stop! Please!" Athena hollered through her sobbing.

Somewhere in pits of what Faith had become she heard her child's small voice trembling for mercy. Faith pulled her arm out of their grasp and laid her head back on the head rest. "Just get me home."

SILENCE FELL between the women at the coffee shop. Faith wiped away the tear that had fallen from her eye. She hated remembering the woman that had terrorized her children. Carol looked at Faith for several minutes. Faith could bare the silence no longer.

"Not the woman you thought I was when you walked in, huh?"

Snapping back to the present moment, Carol watched Faith. "Man, not to be rude, but you were a real. . .well, a real bitch."

"Yes, I was. No denying that reality. I had lost myself."

"What happened after that? Did they press charges? Did Matt want a divorce? I mean, I would have left your crazy ass."

Laughing Faith rubbed her hands through her hair. "No,

they didn't press charges. It was understood that we were both drunk and that things got out of hand. Besides family doesn't rat family out. They just made sure that we were not at the same place at the same time again. As far as Matt is concerned he stayed with me. He just asked me to cut down on the drinking."

"Did you want the divorce? From the way you tell it, it sounds like you did. How come Matt didn't divorce you right then?"

Sighing, Faith took another sip from her coffee. "Yes, I did want the divorce. I can't speak for Matt. I think somewhere he loved me and hoped that the woman he fell in love with would come back."

Confusion spread across Carol's face. "If you wanted the divorce, then why did you stay?"

"I thought I was doing the right thing by the kids. Thought I was doing what the church said to do in marriage. But mostly, if I'm being honest, it was fear."

Carol shifted in her seat obviously still confused. "I don't get it. From what you just said you weren't afraid of anything. I mean you practically beat a woman to death. What could you have possibly been afraid of?"

"Everything. A true drunk is afraid of everything. I was afraid of being on my own. Afraid of losing my kids. Afraid of what people would think."

"But, people divorce all the time. Does anyone even care about that anymore?"

"In my world they did. Very much so."

"What world is that?"

"The religious one."

"Oh, you mean the church world. Sorry, but I just can't see you as the church type. You almost killed someone."

Faith rested her chin on her hands. "I can see why you would be confused, but I lived a double life. By day I was a religious woman who taught kids about God; by night I was a drunk."

"So, what did you do after you got home that day?" Carol gazed over at Faith.

"I slept it off only to wake up that evening and drink again. I apologized to the kids and to Matt, but no one wanted anything to do with me that night. I woke up the next day and went to church like a good little girl and taught those kids like a good little hypocrite. But it would be that next day that would change my life. My God hadn't given up on me yet."

GOD SPEAKS

*M*ake sure you put on your church clothes." Faith hollered at her children through the pounding, relentless hangover that had greeted her when she woke up.

Downing four Advil, her shaking hands fought to carefully put on her make-up in order to hide the bruising the cousin had inflicted through the one punch she managed to lay on Faith.

"Do you even remember what you did yesterday?" Matt was putting on his collared shirt and black slacks.

Pulling on her white sweater over her long blue dress, Faith looked at herself in the mirror. "I remember it in patches. Almost like I'm watching a movie."

"Well it wasn't no damn movie. You scared the hell out of everyone especially the kids. How could you do what you did?"

"Do we really have to go over it again? She started talking crap and I responded. I shouldn't have taken it so far, but what is done is done. Can't say that I'm sorry. She deserved it."

Matt bent over to tie his black shoes. "And you think that you were justified in almost killing a woman before you go to teach the kids at church? Do you seriously not see anything wrong with that?"

Faith moved past Matt to get the kids ready to go to the car. "I don't know what I think about anything right now. I just know we have to get to church, or we are going to be late."

"What does that mean? You don't know what you think about anything?"

Faith whipped around to face him. "It means exactly what I said. I don't know what I think about anything. Alright?! Can we please just get to church?"

"Do you have to bite my head off? Why are you so damn angry all of the time?"

"I just don't want to listen to your crap, or talk about what I'm feeling. I don't know what I'm feeling about anything, alright?"

Matt rolled his eyes. "Kids lets go."

The short drive to church was taken in paralyzing silence. No one dared disturb the dictator.

Why is everyone so quiet? They act like I'm crazy. Like I'm just gonna fly off the handle at any moment. I'm not crazy. I was just drunk and she deserved it.

Faith turned up the radio to interrupt the silence. *Since when are you not drunk?*

I'm not always drunk. I have a job.

Barely.

Doesn't matter. I'm not as bad as they think. She had it coming.

They piled out of the car and into the church's education building. Faith dropped her kids off at their classes smiling and playing her part of the strong good Christian woman who spreads the message of the gospel to all who are willing, and not so willing, to hear. She walked into her classroom full of eighth graders. "Good morning everyone."

"Good morning, Mrs. Smith."

Faith took out her Bible. She had not prepared for the lesson, so she was just going to do the pray and open method of teaching. She said a quick prayer for God's guidance and opened the Bible to a random book. The book of I Peter flopped open. "Today we are going to be talking about (I Peter 5:8)."

The class opened their Bibles to the passage and waited. Faith halted when her eyes fell upon the first two words. They struck her to her core. Slowly she read the passage to the class "Be sober, be vigilant; because your adversary the devil, as a roaring lion, walketh about, seeking whom he may devour."

She stood in silence. All were waiting for her to explain what the passage meant. "Be sober" repeated in her mind bashing over the insides of her skull trying to get her to understand a fact that was just out of reach. She could feel herself on the verge of some breakthrough, some kind of epiphany, but her vision was blurred. Faith knew what "be sober" meant, but she couldn't figure out what it meant for her. *What does being sober mean for me? Is God trying to tell me something?*

"Mrs. Smith?" One of the young students looked up at her waiting for her to respond.

"Yeah, sorry, just got a little lost in thought." Faith put the Bible down and asked the students "What does it mean to be sober?"

She needed to hear their answer more than they needed to learn her answer to the question. A Latino boy spoke up as he normally did during class. He was always eager to learn and more eager to share what his understanding on things were. "It means no alcohol, or drugs."

Faith dug deeper hoping to find an answer to a question she wasn't ready to ask. "Do you think God is calling for us to stay away from alcohol and drugs all the time, or can we dabble a little here and a little there?"

The quiet brunette girl that always sat in the back answered. "Some people can drink a little and be okay. Some can't. I think

God is saying that if you are one of the ones that can't then you have to stay away from it all of the time."

Faith swallowed the lump in her throat that had grown larger with each passing minute since her eyes first fell on those words. Images of yesterday flashed in her memory. "Very good answer. How did you get so smart?"

The girl looked Faith in the eyes and said, "My uncle is an alcoholic and has to stay away from alcohol all of the time, or he winds up doing stupid things. He is one of the ones that can't."

"Wow, I'm glad you shared that with us. So, why do you think God wants us to be sober?" Faith again waited for their answer more than they waited for hers.

The same young man spoke up. "That's simple. So we don't kill ourselves. The devil is the alcohol and drugs that will get ya."

A third child spoke up. He was a talkative kid always with something sarcastic to say. Faith dreaded his input. He smiled a weak smile and spoke. "I think if you're caught up in drugs and alcohol then you can't have true faith. I mean you have faith in what you put your time into. If you are doing drugs and alcohol then your time is in that, so that is where your faith is. If faith is into those things then how can you have faith in God at the same time. I think it's either one, or the other. You can't have both. It doesn't work."

All life came to a stop for Faith. What the sarcastic boy said struck her at her heart. She spent every night drinking. She cancelled plans that got in the way of her drinking. Hell, she had even quit going to Wednesday night Bible study because the class cut into her drinking time. She formed her life around alcohol, not around God. "Another wonderful answer. Y'all have given me much to think about. Sometimes God answers our questions in the most unlikely of places and from the most unlikely of people. I think I'm going to end class a little early today. Y'all have a good week."

The students answered her back. "Bye, Mrs. Smith."

Faith waited for the last student to leave the classroom before she went to the bathroom to collect her thoughts before the church service. Walking into the bathroom, Faith caught a glimpse of herself in the mirror. She hated mirrors. They never lied. They always threw back the truth of what was in front of you the whole time.

She stood there for a few minutes looking at herself the same way she did that morning a few days ago. *Who am I? What am I doing with my life? Maybe I should cut down on drinking. Maybe if I just have a couple of beers instead of the wine then I won't get so tipsy. Maybe I should pick a day of the week and just not drink.*

That last thought stopped her heart. *Just not drink?* That was not even an option. Why should she go a day without drinking when all she was doing was just taking the edge off of the day? Then again why couldn't she not drink for just one day or two? Why did that thought strike more fear in her than she had of God's justice? *I seriously need help.*

A little girl with bright red ribbons in her hair bounced into the bathroom. "Hello, Mrs. Smith."

"Hello." Faith knew the girl from Mary's class. "Is class over?"

"Yeap."

"Okay, thank you." Faith left the bathroom to go pick up her kids and then go to the service.

The hall to the classes was packed with parents and students. Faith gently nudged past the people she felt so distant from. In a hallway full of people, most of whom she knew by name, she felt utterly alone. Inside she held a dark secret that she believed no one else knew. In her mind she held the memory of yesterday along with other memories from over the years that she wished she could forget. How many people had she gotten into fights with? How many fights did she pick with her husband? How many times did she yell at the kids for no real reason?

Countless.

What was the common factor through all those answers? Her drinking. She was always drinking during those times. Hell, even when she was sober, she was so full of rage she thought her brain might split open oozing forth like magma from an angry volcano.

Faith listened to Mary describe her finger painting about Jesus while they walked over to the sanctuary. Once inside, Faith didn't feel at home like some people claimed to feel when they walked in. She suffered a loneliness that she had always experienced, but that today was intolerable. A heavy weight loaded on her shoulders. Her legs were rusted lead pipes that refused to move with ease. Her head could barely hold up against the guilt that had bonded itself to her.

Faith knelt down. She whispered to a God she hoped was truly there with a prayer that she had prayed before, but this time she was spiritually desperate for an answer. "God, help me."

The service went on and ended as it usually did, and Faith just sat as she normally did thinking about the Bible verse she had read earlier. Its meaning trailed her every thought. She had always claimed to believe in scripture, but here was a verse that commanded her to stay sober. Her students understood what that meant, but she had spent her whole life avoiding that verse. She had made countless excuses for why she was living a sober life despite the drinking. Afterall, she didn't do the hard drugs. She had convinced herself that getting drunk everyday was no big deal. Hell she even supported having a few smokes of some good old fashioned Mary Jane. Yet, standing in the middle of those students who defined sobriety in a way that put her in the class of a drunk stabbed at her soul. They knew what that verse meant because they were not looking for reasons to work around it. Her students had taught her.

The family went to lunch as they always did on Sundays. Faith sat consumed with *what was God trying to tell her*. She went home and tried to nap, but the verse kept gnawing at her. Finally, she gave up and went to the living room to watch T.V. Of course, she poured a glass of wine first.

Several glasses of wine later, Faith sat watching a show that held no meaning but passed the time. Mary came up to her with her old worn out blanket in her arms. "Mommy, can I sit with you?"

A part of Faith wanted to embrace her daughter in her arms, to hold on for all she was worth, to love her. Yet, what came out of her mouth shocked her. "Baby, this is mommy time. Go to your dad."

A piece of Faith's soul died as she watched her daughter's face fall and tears form in her eyes. Mary turned clutching onto her blanket and went to her dad. *Why did I say that? Why am I pushing her away?* Faith took a long drink from her glass of wine.

Faith wanted to cry, but the tears refused to come. She took another drink. *God, what is wrong with me? Why did I just do that to my baby? How could I break her heart?*

Oh, come on it's not that bad. So, she went to her dad. That's what he is there for right? Besides this is mommy time. Everyone knows that.

But it isn't right, is it?

What's not right about it? Just drink your wine and enjoy the show.

She drank another glass of wine despite not wanting to. She told herself to stop and to go to bed, but she couldn't. She just kept drinking. Faith sat down in her chair again and reached for her computer. She typed in the search box "Am I an alcoholic?"

To her surprise several pages popped up to answer her question. She chose the site that had a quiz she could take to see if she was an alcoholic.

Answering the questions honestly, Faith hit the submit button. *Surely it will come back and tell me I'm fine. I don't need help.*

The results came up on the screen reading "Severe Alcohol Addiction" and offered several numbers to call for help. *Surely, I answered the questions wrong on this one. I'll take another one.*

Faith went to another website and took another quiz again answering as honestly as she could, and again the results came back advising her to seek immediate help for her alcohol addiction. Once again there were numbers available to call and links to meeting locations. *I'm not an alcoholic, am I?*

One of the numbers on the screen was to a meeting location close to her. *Surely, they are closed. I'll leave a message describing who I am, then they'll call me back tomorrow and leave a message that I'm not a real alcoholic and don't need any help and I can keep drinking.* To her surprise someone answered the phone.

"Hello, this is Brian at A Brighter Tomorrow house. How can I help you?"

Crap! No one was supposed to answer the phone. It's almost 11 p.m. What are they doing answering the phone this late? What do I say?

"Hello?" His calming voice repeated.

Faith finished off the glass of wine she had poured right before she dialed the phone. "Hello. I'm not sure if I'm an alcoholic or not but I drink every day."

Brian's friendly voice answered her back. "I can't tell you if you're an alcoholic or not, but you can come to one of our meetings and find out for yourself. At the very least, you will make a few friends."

What does he mean he can't tell me that I am not an alcoholic?

Make friends? I don't need any flipping friends! Why can't he just tell me that I'm fine?

Faith slurred over her words. "When are your meetings?"

"6:00 p.m. everyday. Come on by."

"Okay, thank you. Bye."

"Have a good night."

"Who the hell were you talking to at this hour?" Matt scared Faith.

Nearly jumping out of her chair, she looked over her shoulder to see Matt coming towards her from the kitchen. "I was just calling someone to see if I'm an alcoholic or not."

Furrowing his eyebrows together, Matt stopped in front of her. "That's stupid. You're not an alcoholic. You just drink too much sometimes."

"But, I drink every day?"

"So? Everyone does that."

"Does everyone get drunk?"

Matt chuckled. "Isn't that the point of drinking? You drink and get a buzz, so what? You're not an alcoholic."

"What about yesterday?"

"What about it. You had a little too much. You're fine."

"I don't know. I just don't feel right. Like maybe I have a problem." Faith gulped from her wine glass.

"If you're that worried about it then stop for a day, or two."

A sudden wrath swept through Faith. "Stop for a day, or two? I don't need to go that far!"

Shocked at the unexpected outburst, Matt stepped back. "Why not? It will give your body a break from the alcohol."

She thought about that simple question. Why couldn't she stop for a day? *Because I don't freaking want to that's why.*

"I don't know, maybe. I'm going to go to bed. I have to be up early for work tomorrow."

Faith climbed into bed and passed out. Her dreamless sleep

left her feeling unrested and hungover when her alarm went off the following morning. She climbed out of bed and took her usual dosage of Advil. That stranger she saw in the mirror last week was staring at her again. For a few moments, Faith stood there staring back at her. The eyes were empty and sad; almost pleading with her to help, but help, she did not know how to get help. *How do I help someone I don't even know and when I don't even know what the problem is?*

The stranger frowned at her. *You know what the problem is. It's obvious. You just don't want to see it. It's the drinking. You need to stop the drinking.*

Faith remembered Brian from the night before. *Maybe I can go to that meeting and see if I'm an alcoholic or not.*

The stranger's mouth turned up slightly. *That's a start. Go to the meeting tonight.*

Faith went to put on her brightly colored patterned dress. She loved the way it made her feel almost happy. Not quite happy, but almost, and that was as close to joy as she was going to get. *I'll think about it. I might go.*

Faith went to the kitchen to get her coffee before waking up the kids. She thanked God that she had finished all the alcohol the night before. *At least I won't be drinking this morning. If I were an alcoholic could I do that? No, I couldn't. I'm not an alcoholic.*

She poured her coffee and went about her morning routine wondering how the day was going to go. Last week was gone, but not the mess she had to deal with at work. Mrs. Lopez was surely still upset with her and she was walking on eggshells with Sanders. She didn't know how to fix things. All she could do was show up to work and do the best she could. No more screw ups.

As they did every morning the little family left the house and headed to the school. Faith felt a mixture of dread and shame. Everything in her life was falling apart. They pulled into the school parking lot at the same time Sanders did. Mary popped up in her seat. "Look, Mom, it's the principal! Let's say 'good morning.'"

"Go ahead baby. I don't think the principal cares to hear from me."

Athena glanced at her mother. "Why not? What happened?"

Pulling her bag and purse over her shoulder, Faith shook her head. "No big deal. I just didn't get something done and she isn't real happy with me. It will work itself out. Nothing to worry about."

"Is that why you were in a bad mood all weekend?"

"I wasn't in a bad mood all weekend."

Athena scoffed. "Is that why you almost killed someone?"

"That was just. . .just whatever. Let's get inside."

Mary swung open the car door. "Good morning, Mrs. Sanders!"

"Good morning, Mary! Hello, Mrs. Smith. How was your weekend?"

Mrs. Sanders was the epitome of class and eloquence. Faith always felt a little like a backwoods hillbilly in a dress when she was around Sanders. "It was fine. How about yours?"

"Not long enough."

They all walked into the school together. The kids went to the auditorium, Sanders to her office, and Faith to her classroom.

"Mrs. Smith."

Faith turned around to see Mrs. Lopez standing at the top of the stairs behind her. She avoided eye contact. She couldn't bear to look Lopez in the face. Faith had always felt inferior to Lopez. Lopez seemed to have everything together and was hard on those who struggled. That was Lopez's flaw: being critical of those who didn't do things the way she thought they should be done. Faith choked over the shame that rattled in her throat. "Good morning. How was your weekend?"

Mrs. Lopez approached Faith. "Considering I had to work all weekend on the HAC it was alright. Listen, I saw you at church yesterday and you didn't look so good. You okay?"

Desperately Faith wanted to tell Lopez all about the weekend and how she thought she might have a drinking problem, but all that would come out of her mouth was "I'm fine. Just a little tired yesterday. Look, I'm real sorry about you getting stuck with the HAC thing."

Lopez waved her off. "Don't worry about it. We all fall down sometimes. You just have to get up and keep going forward. Just come to me before you are in over your head next time."

Relief, sweet precious relief filled Faith's soul allowing her to remember that her and Lopez shared a connection over their faith and that connection had bonded them. Lately, however, Faith couldn't feel that connection. Maybe it was the drinking. Maybe Lopez was trying to reach out to her, but fell short because Faith couldn't see past the wine bottle. She loved Lopez and didn't want to lose her as a friend. "Thank you, I really appreciate that. I don't want to lose you as a friend."

Lopez turned to head back down the stairs. "You aren't going to lose me as a friend. I'm always here for you."

"Thank you. That means a lot to me."

"Oh, I almost forgot. Sanders wants to see you during your conference period today. She asked me to tell you."

"Okay. Thanks." *Now what. What did I do this time?*

Faith spent the rest of the day trying to teach while wondering if she was in trouble again. She racked her brain for the possible reason for the upcoming office visit. Nothing. Nothing came up. She was unprepared for what was coming at her and she didn't like that feeling of no control. Faith liked to at least be prepared for all scenarios, but this one she was clueless.

The sixth period bell rang telling Faith that it was time to see Mrs. Sanders. Slowly she made her way to the office, passing by

Martha the secretary with an automatic, "Hi." The hallway leading to the office seemed to grow longer and more ominous. Finally she stood in front of Sanders' open office door. "Mrs. Sanders? You wanted to see me?"

"Yes, yes I did. Come in and close the door."

This can't be good. Every time she closes the door it's something bad. What the hell did I do this time?

Sanders gestured toward the chairs. "Have a seat."

Faith sat down, with sweaty palms, waiting to hear what Sanders had to say. "I spent all weekend thinking about how you failed at doing your duties on the HAC situation and how all of the responsibility fell upon Lopez. HAC is supposed to teach the students leadership and responsibility. Neither of which you have shown over the last several months. So, I asked myself, if you were one of my students would I just let you walk away without any consequences?"

Sanders paused for a moment. "Well, would I?"

Faith's voice crackled. "No, you wouldn't."

"Correct. So, why would I let one of my teachers get away with such a gross display of bad behavior?"

"You shouldn't." Faith braced herself for whatever punishment was coming next.

"The HAC is a big deal. You dropped the ball that I gave to you. You really let me down, Mrs. Lopez down, and the students down. That can't be tolerated."

"No, it can't."

"I'm taking you off of the HAC team. You will no longer be participating in HAC. I have already asked another teacher to take your spot effective immediately."

Disgusted with herself, Faith sat with her hands folded in on themselves. She deserved what she got. She had let everyone down, and for what? *You already know the answer to that question. Drinking. You let them all down so you could drink.*

"I understand. I'm sorry for letting everyone down."

"I didn't want to have to do this, but you left me with no other option."

Faith fought back tears. "I know. You have to do what you have to do. If I were a student you would have kicked me out of HAC."

Sanders continued. "Remember if anything like this happens again, I will have to write you up."

"Of course."

"I know I have said this before, but please get your act together." Sanders pleaded.

In that moment, Faith knew what she had to do. She had to go to that meeting. What did she have to lose? Maybe someone could help her get control over her drinking. Maybe those people could teach her how to manage her drinking. Faith left Sander's office with her head held down. No joy. No answers. No hope. Just broken.

After school, Faith went to pick up her kids from the auditorium.

"Mom what's wrong?" Athena's voice brimmed with concern.

Faith wanted to lie, but what was the use. Athena was going to find out one way, or another and it might as well be from her. "I'm off the HAC team."

They were getting into the car. "What! Why? What about the upcoming competition?"

Faith numbly put her key in the ignition and sparked the car to life. "I failed at my job. I didn't do what I was supposed to do so I got kicked out. It was my fault. Sanders already found my replacement."

Confusion appeared over Athena's face. "Why didn't you do what you were supposed to do?"

All Faith could answer back was, "I don't know. I really don't know."

Matt was already at home when they pulled into the driveway. Faith knew she had to tell him about HAC and about going to the meeting that evening, but she was sure it would lead to a fight. He was never very understanding and he sure wasn't going to understand her not doing her job.

"Daddy!" Mary squealed with delight as they entered the house.

"Hey, baby. How was your day?"

"Good. Mommy got kicked out of HAC."

Faith's anger boiled over. "Mary! Why did you tell him that?"

Matt studied Faith. "What is she talking about?"

"I didn't prepare for the upcoming HAC and the preparations fell on Lopez. Sanders kicked me off the team because I failed at my responsibilities."

"Why did you do that!? That's your freaking job. Why didn't you handle your business?"

"I don't know why alright! I screwed up. I don't need you yelling at me."

"Well someone needs to. What the hell is wrong with you? You could have gotten fired."

Fuming, shaking, and flushed Faith spoke through her gritted teeth. "I. Do. Not. Need you yelling at me or correcting me."

"Obviously, you need someone to correct you. You're screwing up and to put that on Lopez is just a crappy thing to do. Man, that is really shitty of you."

"You think I don't know that? You think I don't have guilt over that? I really don't need you in my face lecturing me about how I screwed up."

Matt didn't let the issue go. "I just don't get how you let this happen. I can't do that at my job. What makes you think you can do that at your job?"

"You're like a dog with a bone. You never let anything go. Just drop it already. Just leave me alone."

Disgusted with herself, Matt, and the whole conversation, she turned to walk away and remembered the meeting. "Oh, and I'm going to a meeting tonight about my drinking."

Puzzled, Matt asked, "What the hell for? I thought we talked about this last night. You're not an alcoholic."

"I'm not so sure about that. I think I have been drinking too much lately. I think I might need some help dealing with it. You have even said that I needed to slow down and maybe take a day, or two off."

He pulled out his laptop and set it on the counter. "Whatever. If you think you need help go, but I'm telling you that you're fine. Sure you should take a day off once in a while for health reasons and maybe watch how much you drink at parties, but it's nothing I can't help you manage. Going to a meeting trying to fit in with a bunch of drunks who have been arrested and are homeless because of drinking is just you being dramatic as usual."

Faith watched him pull up his work emails. Confused and angry she wanted to scream at him, to shake him, to tell him that something was terribly wrong. She didn't quite know what that wrong was, but she was losing a battle. The trick was she couldn't describe that battle because she wasn't sure what she was fighting. All she knew for certain was that she couldn't keep going the way she was. Something had to change. "I'm not being dramatic. I just need to. . .I feel like. . .I don't know. . .I just need to go. I feel like I'm losing control."

Looking up from the computer, he shrugged his shoulders. "Then go. Are you going to have dinner with us?"

"You know I don't eat dinner, but there is the pot roast in the crock pot that is ready. All that needs to be done is to eat it. The veggies and potatoes cooked with the meat. I'm going to go lay down for a few minutes."

"You're not even going to sit with us? The kids want to spend time with you."

A pinch of guilt twisted in Faith's stomach. "Not tonight. I will tomorrow."

"You always say that. Whatever. Go do what you want like you always do. Everything is always about you."

Faith went to her room and shut the door. Dishes clamored in the kitchen. Children's voices echoed through the house. The occasional laugh from the dinner table stabbed at her soul. Alone. She was utterly alone no matter where she was.

This is hell. I'm in hell and there is no way out. Why am I like this? Why can't I be like everyone else? What is so wrong with me that I can't seem to function in this world? Why do I abandon my family?

Minutes ticked by while Faith laid adrift in her bed. She kept thinking about the last thing Matt said. Everything was about her and she didn't know why. *Where did everything go wrong?* Eventually, the hour came for her to go to the meeting. Her nerves began to tremble. Her heart beat a little faster. She gathered up what little courage she had and left her bed. At the front door, she turned around to look at her husband. She was still angry at him, but she wished he would go with her. "Do you want to go?"

Matt scoffed. "Hell, no I don't want to go. Why would I go? I don't drink."

"It's just that..."

"Just what?"

I need you. For the first time in a long time I need you. I can't do this on my own. "Never mind. I'll see you when I get back."

"Okay. Have fun?"

A snicker broke away from Faith. "Hardly. Bye."

She pulled into the packed parking lot of the meeting place. *Crap. There are so many people here. I do NOT want to do this.*

Maybe I should just go home. No. I came this far. I can go in sit down and just get through the hour. Maybe no one will notice me. Why are there so many people standing outside?

Several people stood on a porch that wrapped around the building. Most of them were smoking. She turned off the car watching the people she didn't want to meet. They were laughing, talking. They seemed happy. *They seem nice enough. Just walk up there and go inside. They aren't going to bite.*

Faith walked with her head down not wanting to make eye contact with anyone. She could feel eyes moving over her. There was a door behind a group of men who were talking while eyeing her up and down. *That must be the way in. Just go through the door and sit down. No one will notice you. It's just an hour of your time.*

She opened the door and went inside a faux wood paneled room lined with white tables and chairs. More people were sitting inside than were standing outside. People turned to glance her way. *Great. More freaking people. Just gonna sit in the middle chair and be quiet. No one will notice me. I'll listen then bolt the hell out of here.*

She sat on the hard chair. She stared at her fidgeting hands. Not wanting to look up. Not wanting to make eye contact, not wanting to talk to anyone, she sat. A painting of a man sitting on a bed talking with two well-dressed men hung on the wall. Faith didn't know what the painting meant, but she instinctively knew that she was the man on the bed. *Who are the men he is talking to and what are they saying?"*

"Hi, my name is Tina."

Faith jumped in her seat. A dark-haired woman kneeled in front of her. The only thing that Faith could get out of her mouth was "My husband says I'm not an alcoholic, so I don't think I belong here."

Tina didn't flinch. "Okay. Do you want to come sit with me

over there?" She pointed to the back of the room where there were even more people. *My God, how many people come here?*

Faith picked up her purse. "Okay."

Tina's petite frame bounced in front of Faith who felt like Godzilla stomping through Tokyo. Sometimes she hated being so tall. Her height made it impossible to hide, or to blend in. They sat at a table that faced the rest of the room. Tina motioned for Faith to sit. Faith did as she was summoned.

Tina looked Faith in the eyes. "People trying to discover if they are an alcoholic or not, tend to always listen for the differences in order to cling to the idea that their drinking isn't that bad. So, listen for the similarities. You may be surprised at what you find."

She pushed a book towards Faith. "We read from this."

This meeting comes with a book? Damn what have I gotten myself into? Do these people seriously not drink? What the hell do they have to be so damn happy about? They gotta be on something. No one is this damn happy without some kinda help.

Tina knocked on the table to begin the meeting. Throughout the whole meeting Faith grew in confidence that she was not an alcoholic because she wasn't as bad as any of these crazy people that spoke. Many had been arrested, some had lost everything, others had DUIs. Faith was just about to pat herself on the back for being normal and put together when one woman spoke. One woman's story matched her own. One woman hit a nerve. One woman read Faith's story to her.

Her words were simple. She couldn't pass by a wine bottle without drinking the whole thing. She could never say no to a drink. She had still had a job and a place to live when she admitted she was an alcoholic. For her, the bottom was a spiritual and emotional chaotic hell that consumed her mind. That woman spoke Faith's truth.

BROKEN DOLL

*T*he meeting ended with Faith knowing she was going to go home and drink. It was all she was thinking about the whole meeting, but that woman's story floated around in her thoughts. *If she is an alcoholic then so am I.*

I can't be an alcoholic. I just can't be. I don't want to be one of those people. I mean they never drink again. Never. That's a damn long time.

Faith stood with Tina on the porch and smoked a cigarette. Several women came up to Faith and gave her their phone numbers and told her that everything was going to be okay, but Faith was breaking further. She was crying on the inside. Something was dying inside of her, but she didn't know what it was, or what it meant. Something was giving way. Giving way to what? Faith didn't know.

She left with a paper of phone numbers in her hand and a tear running down her cheek. She drove home in silence. No thoughts but the memory of the stories from the meeting. No plans but to drink that wine waiting for her on the kitchen counter. No explanations except that she was losing control, or maybe she never really had control. Maybe control was all an illusion and her illusions were crumbling away through her fingers.

She walked through the front door to see Matt sitting on the couch working on his computer. He looked over the screen. "So, are you an alcoholic?"

Faith ignored him and went straight to the kitchen to her blessed bottle of red wine. She poured herself a glass. Matt came up from behind her. "Well? Are you?"

She took a long drink from her glass. The warm release rushed over her. "I'm pretty sure I am."

"Of course, you are, according to them. They need more people, so they brainwash you into thinking that you are one of them."

Faith rolled her eyes. "It's not like that."

"So, what are you going to do? Stop drinking?"

She walked away from him to go outside. She needed air. She needed to breathe. Faith sat under her favorite oak tree in the back yard. The final days of winter were giving way to the warmth of spring. A flick of the lighter lit her cigarette. She deeply inhaled the smoke that she hoped would one day kill her. Matt had followed her outside waiting for her to answer his question. Finally, Faith answered. "I don't know. I just don't know."

The night passed in front of her like pictures of a movie. She sat in front of the T.V not seeing, not hearing. The kids came in and went out. She mumbled, but comprehended nothing. More wine. More beer. She kept the list of numbers in her hand. Her phone laid next to her. Tina's number stood out above the rest. Tired of the battle she didn't know she was fighting, Faith picked up her phone and dialed in Tina's number. She couldn't call. What would she say that wouldn't sound like the drunk she was. She texted with the only words she could manage to say.

"I'm drinking again."

Faith put the phone down believing that no way in hell she would get a response at this late hour. Who would answer the rambling of a drunk who was a stranger?

Her phone vibrated. A text message waited for her to read. *She actually responded? Holy shit!* Faith read the text.

"Thank you for being honest. Do you want to stop?"

Faith began to cry. "I can't. I just can't. Does that make me an alcoholic?"

Tina responded quickly. "Meet me before the meeting tomorrow."

"Okay."

"Try to go sleep it off and I'll see you tomorrow."

"Okay."

"You aren't alone." Tina's last text made Faith cry harder. Was it true? Was she really not alone? Could those people really understand where she was coming from? Could they really help make the world stop spinning?

Faith woke up before the alarm and sat on the edge of the bed waiting for the pounding in her head to ease. She knew what she was going to do. Nothing mattered anymore. She was done fighting. To stop was impossible. That much she knew. The people at the meeting spoke of how difficult it was. She couldn't stop, and she couldn't pretend that she was normal.

She was a broken doll that had been cast away into the trash. She went straight to the kitchen, took out the bottle of beer, popped it open and drank it all as fast as she could. She grabbed another one popped it open and took a drink. Grabbing her cigarettes she went outside to smoke under the tree she would sometimes imagine hid her from the eyes of God. Hiding from him is what made that big beautiful oak her favorite place to sit and to just let the waves of the abyss come take her away.

She texted her boss and said she was sick and would not be into work that day. She was just going to stay home and drink until she died. There was nothing left to live for. Her marriage was a disaster. Her job was a prison that was about to throw her out with the rest of the garbage. She was damaging her children. What did she have to live for? She thought of Tina. She remembered what Tina said. "You're not alone."

Another long drag to fry her lungs, Faith decided to cancel meeting Tina before the meeting. Nothing and no one could help her. She put out her cigarette and went inside to find her phone. She passed by her kids' rooms. They were asleep and she planned to keep them that way for as long as they would stay in the fields of dreams. No sense in waking them to the nightmare that was unfolding before their eyes.

She grabbed her phone and found Tina's number. "I can't meet you tonight. It's pointless. Fuck it. Fuck it all. Thanks for trying."

Faith didn't expect a response this early, but she heard her phone vibrate. She picked it up and felt her eyes burn with tears. "Can you meet me now?" Was all that Tina texted.

Fighting back the tears, Faith responded. "I can't. I have the kids."

"Why aren't they going to school?"

Faith answered truthfully for the first time in a long time. For the first time in many years, Faith declared the truth. "Because I don't want to pick them up from school drunk. I plan on drinking all day."

The phone started to ring. *Shit. Why is she calling? I don't want to talk. Crap, crap, crap!* Faith answered the phone. "Hello?"

A stern voice replied. "You drinking now?"

"Yes."

"Stop, just for now. Get the kids up. Take them to school. Meet me at the club after you drop them off. Just don't drink till then. Okay?"

Faith wanted to cling to her plan, but the child within cried out to her to, begged her to stop killing them. That child begged her to meet Tina. She listened to the child. "Okay."

Faith woke up the kids. No yelling, just the weak ramblings of a defeated woman hoping that her kids would sense her descent into the flames of hell and would, for once, just do what they were told. To her surprise, they did. All of them woke up and got dressed.

Athena hugged her mom as they were leaving to go to school. Matt still slept. "It's going to be okay, Mom. I promise."

Faith pulled Athena into her chest. "I hope so, baby."

After she dropped off the kids, she drove to the club with her thoughts racing round and round like a rat on a wheel. She pulled into the same parking lot that had greeted her the night before. One car waited for her. She assumed that this was Tina's car. She pulled her car next to the new white SUV.

Tina waited for her on the porch. Faith got out of the car careful to grab her cigarettes. She walked up the ramp to the porch and approached Tina in quiet reflection. She was walking into the unknown with only another drunk to help her.

Tina spoke first. "I'd ask how you are, but I can tell by looking at ya that you have seen better days. You look like hell."

"Thanks." Faith's sarcasm hid the shame she felt for having already had a couple of drinks. "I've been better."

"So, tell me what brought you in to the meeting last night."

Faith just sat there unable to speak, to move. Tina glanced over at her with a sad knowing look. "Do you want some coffee? There is some inside. You can have as much as you can drink."

"That sounds good." Faith opened the door leading into the meeting room to find the coffee. The large room was quiet and empty unlike the night before. The coffee pot stood like a beacon on a dark night in the kitchen that was located at the far side of the building. Grabbing a styrofoam cup, Faith filled it with coffee and walked back out onto the porch where Tina was smoking.

Lighting her cigarette, Faith answered Tina's question. "I need help with my drinking, but I don't know if I'm an alcoholic."

"When you start drinking can you stop?"

"Not really, I mean I have a limit of drinks I allow myself."

"Do you stick to that limit?"

"Not always. In fact, if I'm being honest, I often go over the limit I set, but I do stop drinking by midnight 'cause I have to get up and go to work."

Tina nodded her head. "Have you ever tried to stop drinking and found that you couldn't go without it?"

Faith chuckled the laugh of a condemned man trying to ease the pain of his conviction. "I can't even go a day without it. I've tried and it was an awful experience."

"So, do you think you are an alcoholic?"

It was a simple question that required only a simple yes or no answer, but Faith sat on the hard, white chair paralyzed in a suffocating fear. What did it really mean to be an alcoholic anyway? What if she wasn't and she was just a dumb drunk who couldn't get her act together for whatever reason?

"I think I am."

"Then what are you going to do about it?"

Do about it? What did one do about it? But Faith knew the answer to that question no matter how hard she tried to run from the answer. "Stop drinking?"

Tina's eyes never left Faith's. Her eyes bore into Faith's soul with a wisdom that Faith could only dream of having. "Yeap. There is a ladies meeting soon. I want you to go to it. You need to meet some women who have sobriety."

Conquered by the beast that was eating her alive, Faith relented herself into the care of a stranger. "Okay."

For the next hour Faith listened to Tina's story. She tried to find all of the differences between them because she didn't want to be like Tina. She didn't want to be an alcoholic who had to go the rest of her life without drinking. The differences were obvious. Faith had never been arrested. Never lost a job. Still had her marriage. Never had a DUI. Yet, there was one glaring similarity that Faith could not pretend away: the alcohol was always at the center of all the troubles. Alcohol was the villain in both of their stories. Except, Faith was stronger and was beginning to believe that maybe she wasn't an alcoholic like Tina. Sure, Faith had a drinking issue, but it was manageable. Right?

Tina looked at her watch. "It's almost time for the meeting. Let's go."

Faith had noticed the women going into the building while Tina spoke. A few even came up to Tina to say hello. She had introduced Faith to each woman who looked at Faith with knowing sympathy. Faith followed behind Tina into the room.

Faith's stomach twisted. Her palms became clammy. Sweat began to drip from her armpits. She looked towards Tina. "I need to use the restroom."

Tina pointed to the hallway leading away from the kitchen. Faith followed her hand and found the ladies restroom that was painted a pale blue color with placards that read "Love Yourself" adorning the walls. Faith glared at the stranger that stalked her every step and was always there in the mirror seeming to mock her. She didn't recognize the woman. No makeup. Hair in a messy bun. Clothes wrinkled. Dead eyes. Faith wanted to put the mask on, but she couldn't find the energy to find it and put it on. *I am who I am.* She talked to the angry reflection. *If I'm an alcoholic then I'm an alcoholic. I can't keep going. I can't keep pretending. But how do I stop drinking?* The angry woman answered back. "Go find out."

Faith stepped into the meeting that was already underway.

She sat next to Tina. Each woman told her story. Each story Faith found the differences. But just as there was the night before there was one woman with one story that shook the very foundations Faith stood on. Her story was Faith's story almost word for word. Like Faith she had never been arrested or had DUIs, but there she was—an alcoholic. Deep down inside, where the child was drowning, something snapped and broke into a thousand pieces. Faith frantically tried to gather the pieces and to put them back, but she couldn't make them fit. Nothing would fit together. Damn it, the pieces didn't match. They wouldn't go back together. Sobs from the dying self erupted from the core of Faith's being. No more could she hold back the flood gates. No more could she run. No more could she hide from the stranger in the mirror. The time had come to face the demons she had been running from. Tears poured from her eyes.

Another woman another story that was filled with similarities to Faith. More tears. Tissue after tissue fell upon the table. Tina's hand stroked her back. The women in the room gently smiled in recognition of her pain. They had been there and their smiles told her that they got through to the other side of hell. Faith prayed for death. *How did I get to this point? How am I here? What the hell happened?*

The meeting had come to an end. The woman leading the meeting was handing out chips. The first one was called a desire chip that was available for anyone wishing to stop drinking for 24 hours. Faith knew she needed one. She wanted it, but how was she going to go that long without a drink? A ragging battle gashed at her insides. *Get it. We are dying. Go get it.*

Wait. Why would you want to do that? There is nothing wrong with enjoying a few drinks. You are not an alcoholic.

Yes, you are. For God sakes can't you see? Keep drinking and you will lose everything. Keep drinking and you will die. Take the damn chip. Walk forward. Stop falling backwards into torment. Stop believing the lie because it's easier.

For too long, Faith had traveled alone in the darkness. Here in the room full of women was a little light. Faith wanted that light with all of her being. Slowly, she pulled herself up and walked to the woman who opened her arms to Faith. Tears streamed from her eyes and fell upon the woman's shoulder as Faith took the tiny chip into her hands.

"You can do this. One day at a time." The woman's eyes held the same wisdom that Tina's did.

Faith walked back to her seat unable to stop the tears. She didn't want to drink ever again, but didn't want to live without alcohol. How could she live without alcohol?

After the meeting, the women came up to Faith assuring her that life is worth living. Life is more beautiful without alcohol. One day at a time. This feeling will pass. All of their words crashed against her and fell to the ground that was saturated with her tears.

Tina pulled Faith to the side. "You need to call into work for the next couple of days. Tell them you have the flue if you want, but you need some time off while you detox."

Panic settled over Faith. "Detox? I can't miss work. I'm in enough trouble as it is."

Firmly, Tina answered Faith. "Your body will go through withdrawals from not having the alcohol. In fact, I'm not too sure you shouldn't go to a detox center. As far as your job is concerned, you will not be able to work while you detox. You can get into a bit of trouble now, or continue drinking and lose your job and everything else. Up to you."

"I can't afford a detox center."

"Your job's insurance will probably pay for it, but you would have to come clean to your boss."

"Not happening. I don't want anyone to know that I'm an alcoholic. I'll detox at home."

Tina scoffed. "No, you won't. You'll detox with me and another woman. You can't detox alone. It's too dangerous both physically and mentally. For the next three days, we are attached at the hip. Those cravings are going to hit, and they are going to hit hard."

Fear fingered its way into Faith's mind. She hadn't thought that far ahead. She hadn't considered that her body would have a say in the matter. She just kind of assumed that her body would be grateful. Now she finds out her body is going to have a major temper tantrum that may threaten her sobriety. "Okay. So will we hang out here?"

"We will make every meeting that they have. In between meetings we will be at my house. I will be watching you closely to see if we need to take you to the hospital."

Shock. Horror. More fear engulfed Faith. She twisted her fingers around each other. "Wait. What? Hospital?"

Serious eyes blinked back at Faith. "You have been drinking hard for over 20 years. Do you honestly think that your body is just going to let that go without a fight? Your body is dependent on the alcohol just to function normally. Now you are going to take that way and expect it to function on its own. It's going to protest and that can be medically dangerous. You may have to have medical intervention."

Faith felt like a brick just swung down and whacked her across the head. *Is all this precaution really necessary? Isn't this all a bit over the top? It's just alcohol.*

As if reading her mind, Tina broke Faith's thoughts. "Alcohol is a dangerous drug. Make no mistake it will kill just like any other drug except it will rob you of everything first."

"Holy shit."

"'Holy shit' indeed. This shit is serious."

Gone were the days of college parties. Here were the days of life and death. If she continued to drink she would die. If she stopped she could get very ill. *Damned if I do; even more damned if I don't. Just how did I get into this shit storm?*

Tina picked up her purse. "Come on. You are coming with me to my house. Find someone to pick up your kids from school. Have you told your husband what you're doing?"

Faith couldn't help but laugh. She had forgotten all about Matt. "No, didn't even think to tell him. He doesn't think I'm an alcoholic."

Tina furrowed her eyebrows as she got into the SUV. "One issue at a time. First step is getting you through these next few days. Call him and tell him what you are doing and that you are going to be hanging with me for the time being. If he needs to talk to me, that's fine."

Faith begrudgingly dialed his number. She knew he would not approve of her taking time off of work. He wouldn't approve of any of this. "Hello?"

"Hey Matt, I'm with Tina from that meeting I went to. I've decided to quit drinking and she says that I will be detoxing and need to take a few days off of work."

A few moments of silence passed between them. "What the hell are you doing this for? You are in enough trouble at work. You can't miss work. For god sakes, Faith, you are not an alcoholic. Just go home and I'll meet you there. We can talk about this."

Annoyance threatened to evolve into a wrath that could strike fear into demons. Faith had fought like hell to get to this point; to take that chip. And now he is going to threaten that because why? Why couldn't he see that she was a drowning woman? Why couldn't he see how miserable she was? "No, I'm doing this. I can't drink anymore."

"Fine. If you don't want to drink that's fine, but you don't need that group. I'll help you."

Pure fury erupted from Faith. "Why are you doing this? You've seen how much I drink. You know how I am when I don't drink? Why can't you see that I have a problem? I need help."

Rage met rage. Matt yelled back at her. "Why are you like this?! You are so dramatic. You don't need a group to help you. You just want the attention they give you. If you need help I can help you. I won't let you drink."

Her soul ached at the touch of his words. Was she just being dramatic? Was she just after the attention? Was she even an alcoholic? Maybe he was right. Maybe she was just insane and needed the attention.

Tina extended her hand and motioned for Faith's phone. Defeated Faith handed her the phone.

Her voice was filled with a no nonsense tone. She knew no fear. She stood on firm ground. Faith was jealous of her big-lady balls. "Hello, this is Tina. I'm the one helping your wife get sober. She is an alcoholic and needs the help of other alcoholics. I realize that this is a scary time for you as well, but she needs to do this before she dies. Trust me the drinking will only get worse and you will lose her to the alcohol if she doesn't stop now.

"She will be with me during the day and with you at night. She is going to need your support tonight and tomorrow night and probably for the next several nights. The cravings and withdrawals will be brutal and she is going to need all of the support she can get. Thank you for understanding. We are on our way to my house. You'll see her tonight after the meeting."

Tina hung up the phone without hearing any protest he could possibly muster up. "We will deal with your marriage in time, but know this, no changes in anything for a while. Your number one priority is staying sober."

Faith watched the world slide by the passenger window. She didn't know where she was, or where she was going and for the first time she didn't care.

"YOUR HANDS ARE SHAKING. YOU OKAY?" Faith examined Carol the same way Tina had done in those early days.

Carol clenched her hands into fists. "I'm fine."

Faith knew why she shook. "How long has it been since your last drink?"

Small tears gathered in the corner of her eyes. "Um, I don't know, uh, I guess it's been about 12 hours now."

"Good for you. Half way through your first 24 hours. You should be proud."

Carol wiped away the runaway tear that cut through her dirt caked face. "Did you have bad withdrawals that day?"

Faith shook her head and laughed. "I felt like I was losing my mind. Thinking back I think I was losing my mind—my alcoholic mind. It fought me. It didn't want to let me go. There I was laying on a stranger's living room floor shaking, sweating, and crying for a drink. Do you know what I was thinking?"

Carol nodded.

"I was thinking that I was just being dramatic like Matt had said and that all I needed was one glass of wine. I wasn't a real alcoholic because all I needed was one drink. Just the one and I'd be alright. Sick. Just sick."

Carol whispered in a voice that shook like her hands. "How long did the detox last?"

"The first three days were the worst. I couldn't eat, couldn't sleep, couldn't get comfortable. My body felt like it was on fire as my nerves felt everything for the first time in years. It was like a thousand fire ants biting my legs to my feet. My feet would cramp up and curl in on themselves. It was painful. I cried. At one point, I put my shoes on ready to go to the corner store to get some cheap wine and end my suffering. I was lightheaded. Instead, I slumped down onto my bedroom floor and prayed to God to help me."

"And did he?"

"I'm sitting here, aren't I?"

Again, Carol nodded. "How did your husband react? Was he helpful?"

Faith hesitated. She wanted to be done with the subject of her husband, but there were some truths that can't be hidden because the truth comes out no matter much dirt is used to bury it. "No, he was never helpful. He offered to buy me beer. He kept saying I wasn't an alcoholic."

"How about today. Does he see it now?"

"Nope, in fact he goes around telling everyone that I'm not a real alcoholic, but that is an issue for later in the story. He had his own issues to deal with and I wasn't helpful to him in anyway."

Carol fiddled with her fingers again. "So, how did you manage to stay sober?"

Riotous laughter burst from Faith. "Grace of God. I did everything possible to screw up my sobriety. In fact, I'm a walking talking version of what not to do in this program. I hadn't stopped being a tornado. All I did was put the drink down. At first, I didn't do anything to change the actions I was living. In short: I was a mess."

JUST KEEP GOING

*W*hat do you see when you see me? A lost little girl you need to provide correction to? Am I a woman fighting for her life? Or, maybe, just maybe I'm your little girl that you need to control and you don't want me to wake up from the stupor I have been sinking in for years?"

Matt's face contorted into a scowl. "What the hell are you talking about? I see you as my wife, my very confused wife."

Faith blinked at him and let out a long sigh. "You're right. I'm very confused, but one thing I do know is that I can't drink no matter how hard you try to make me."

Faith now regretted not staying with Tina while she went through this withdrawal. She had wanted the comfort of her home and thought that Matt would be supportive. Even after all he had said she thought he would respect her decision to be sober. She told Tina he would be a good source of support. She now knew that she was wrong. He didn't want her sober. He didn't want her thinking about life. He wanted her drunk.

"I'm not trying to make you drink. I'm trying to get you to see that you are not an alcoholic and that you don't need those people to help you. I can help you."

Scoffing, Faith lifted herself up from the bed. Her legs were burning down to her feet. "How is offering to go get me beer helping me?"

"You need it. Some people just need a little alcohol to get through the day. There is nothing wrong with that."

Tina had been right. She had a keen awareness that most spouses of alcoholics are enablers to the addiction. Their reasons for enabling may vary, but they all give way to the addiction in some form. Faith wished she had listened to Tina.

Faith hung her and head and shook it back and forth unable to believe the words coming out of Matt's mouth. "Do you hear yourself? Some people need it? Those people are called alcoholics. Why can't you see that I'm an alcoholic? Why can't you support me? Why are you fighting me on being sober?"

Matt sat in silence as Faith's gaze refused to let go of him. "I don't want to lose you."

Faith got up and began to walk out of the room. "You are already losing me. You have been losing me for a long time. I'm trying to find my way home and you are trying to ruin that."

Sadness fell over Matt. His voice trembled on the verge of tears. "I'm not trying to ruin anything. I'm just trying to find my wife."

She stopped in the doorway. Pieces of her heart broke over his defeated tone.

A small part of me wants to run into his arms and bury my head in his chest.

Faith clutched her fists. *No, too much had been said over the years. My heart has hardened against him. Too much had been done to break the binds of marriage. I just can't.*

Faith's heart had turned cold toward her husband. *I wish it wasn't so, but I can no longer deny the reality. I can't pretend anymore. The love is dead.*

Maybe not. Maybe there is some thread still there.

No, all the blame is on him. He is too controlling. His words are like knives slashing open my heart. He is just mean.

Oh, come on now. You know you had a part to play in this mess. Deep down inside she knew that she was just as guilty as him for the failure of the marriage.

It's not like you've been easy to live with. Didn't you pick fights with him to stroke your own ego; to prove you were right? Haven't you torn at his heart the way he has torn at yours?

Faith wanted to turn to face him to apologize for her part, but too many memories of things done and said spun through her mind. *No. it's too late. It's only a matter of time before we divorce. It breaks my heart, but there is really nothing that can be said to save this marriage.*

The life she had pictured for herself as a child was gone and she was just as much to blame as anyone else. Maybe even more to blame.

Two weeks passed in a blur. Faith went to meetings and hung out with Tina when she wasn't at work. Each passing day the withdrawals grew weaker, but something else was growing in magnitude. She didn't understand what was transpiring, but she felt like a tidal wave was crashing down around her.

After a week, she went back to work as a zombie. She was physically there, but mentally absent. People around her looked at her with concern, but no one asked if she was alright. No one asked if they could help. No one reached out a hand. Not Lopez. Not Sanders. Not anyone. Faith was standing in the void, chains unlocked, but no ability to move. Had one person asked if she was okay, she may have told them the truth. Had one person extended a hand to help pull her up she would have grabbed onto it for dear life, but no one did. Everyone had backed away when she needed them the most. People she thought would have her back no matter what had disappeared. So, on and on she went, no longer numb, but no longer able to cope.

Her alarm went off again. Faith turned it off and sat on the edge of the bed feeling as if life had left her behind. *I can't do this anymore.* Sluggishly she got up and went to the kitchen unsure of where her feet were taking her, but knowing that her mind was tearing away from reality. She pulled open a drawer that held the knives. She grabbed the butcher knife and stared at the shiny blade. *Remember you have to cut deep enough to hit a vein, or it won't work.*

She placed the blade along her blue vein gently sliding it up and down her wrist. *There would be a lot of blood. Maybe I should do this in the bathroom.*

What about the kids? Do you really want them to find you dead in the bathroom?

No, no that would be bad. I could take them to school and then jump off that bridge that is so high. There would be no way I could survive the fall. Anyway, slitting the wrists is no guarantee of death.

Jumping though. That would be a guarantee.

Faith returned the knife to its place in the drawer. Several minutes passed as she stood in the kitchen looking out the window above the sink. Little fat happy birds fluttered through the oak trees that lined the street. *I wish I was one of those birds. I want to fly.*

You can fly. Right off that bridge. Just jump and all of your pain will be done.

What about hell? Don't people who commit suicide go to hell?

Come on no one knows that. Surely God knows how much pain you're in. He'll understand.

Faith stood in the kitchen for several more minutes now looking at the coffee maker, unable to find the energy to make the coffee that she so cherished, and unable to stop the images of her flying to her death. "Mom?"

Athena stood in the middle of the kitchen staring at her mother. Faith barely lifted her head. "Yes?"

Athena cautiously walked closer to her. "You okay? You look weird just standing there."

Faith's eyes brimmed with tears. "No. No I'm not okay."

Athena wrapped her small arms around Faith's waist and laid her head on her mother's chest. "Maybe you should call that lady. I can't remember her name. She goes to the meetings with you."

"Tina?"

"Yeah. Call her."

"I'll call her during my lunch break."

Gently, Athena pulled away. Whatever it is, it's going to be okay. Just keep going."

Faith wiped away a tear. "I'm trying. I'm really trying."

Once again, Faith went to work and fought like hell to get through the day with as many smiles as she could muster. All day the images of her jumping darted through her mind. *What about your students? Don't they matter? What would they think if you offed yourself?*

They might be a little sad, but they are better off without me. They need a more focused teacher; not a screw up like me.

But you love to teach. Grab onto that.

I used to love teaching, but right now I don't want to be here in this classroom. It's a reminder of my failures.

More and more she felt that to jump was to escape the inner death she already felt. Yet, every once in a while images of Athena flashed before her eyes. Athena asked her to keep going, so she must try to keep going. During her lunch break, she stayed behind in her classroom to call Tina.

Immediately, Tina answered the phone. "Hey, girl. What's going on?"

Faith thought of several lies she could tell, but what was the point of lying? She needed to tell the truth if she was ever going to get through whatever it was that she was dealing with. "The truth is that I'm not doing so hot. I'm not sure what's wrong with me, but I don't want to do anything, or go anywhere. I am so sad and I don't know why. I feel like I'm drowning. What do I do?"

Tina sighed through the phone. "What you are going through is normal. You are mourning the loss of your best friend, your only solution to all your problems. You are mourning the death of your old life. Just keep doing what you are doing. This too will pass."

Faith wasn't so sure that was the only thing wrong with her. It made sense and she was sad over the loss of alcohol, but the sorrow was so deep she could feel its fingernails in her soul. "I have something else I need to tell you."

"Go ahead."

She paused for a moment unwilling to spew out what she was really thinking, but she had little choice. There was a war splitting her into pieces and she couldn't keep fighting forward. Faith was losing the will to live. "I don't want to live anymore. I have no desire to keep going. Like zero."

"Well, that is something else entirely. Are you suicidal?"

Silence. She intertwined her fingers. The pit of her stomach burned. How does one tell anyone that they wish to end their life? It's not like you just walk up to someone and say 'Hey, I want to slit my wrists today because life is too much for me to handle.' How do you say the words that no one wants to hear and even fewer actually understand? But Faith had little choice. It was either confess, or die. She had reached the end of the road. The darkness was overwhelming. That little light she saw a few weeks ago was gone. No light existed in her world. No joy. No hope. She was just treading water in a black sea on a black night. "Yes, yes I am."

"Okay. I want you to leave work after your last class and meet me at the club. I'm going to make some phone calls to see if I can get you in to see a psychiatrist, or a hospital."

Terror struck Faith. "I can't miss any work. I'm on thin ice here. I could be written up."

A drill sergeant's voice answered her back. "You don't have a choice. You are in a depression that you cannot pull out of on your own. You need help. You are going to have to come clean to your boss. You need to let her know everything that is going on with you and you need to do it today. Meet me at the club immediately after work."

"Okay." Faith hung up the phone and looked out the window. *I thought when I quit drinking everything would be better, but hell everything is worse. How am I here in this chair praying for death? What is wrong with me?*

During her conference period, Faith went to Sander's office to reveal everything to her. There was no use in hiding anymore. She was fracturing into a thousand pieces and if she didn't reach out for help she may not find the ability to put herself back together again. She walked through the door and found Sanders busy at her desk. "I'm sorry to bother you, but we need to talk."

Sanders looked up from her computer. "Of course. What do you need to talk about?"

Fiddling with her fingers as she did when she was nervous, Faith sat down in the chair. "I need to be honest with you about what is going on in my life because I think I may be in some serious trouble."

Sanders closed her computer then got up to close her office door. Quietly she sat back down and waited for Faith to continue.

Faith tucked a loose strand of hair behind her ear. "I'm an alcoholic. I am 21 days sober and am experiencing a severe depression that I can't seem to get out of. A friend of mine thinks I need professional help. I don't know if I do or not. All I know is that I'm not well and I don't know how to fix it. It's like I have lost the road I was driving on and am now stuck on this back woods road with no map and no road signs to tell me where to go. I'm scared."

Sanders sat considering what Faith had just revealed. She leaned forward on her desk with her chin resting upon her folded hands. "I knew something was wrong. I'm glad you are getting the help you need for your alcoholism. Whatever I can do to help you I will do. I care for you and want to see you get through this. Do you need to take some time off?"

Relief fell over Faith. She eased back into the chair allowing the muscles in her back to relax. "I don't know. I hope not. I'm supposed to meet with my friend after school and see if she was able to get me into a psychiatrist."

"Well if you need time off, let me know. I want to help, but you have to let me help you. I can't help if I don't know what's wrong. You will get through this."

"Thank you. I appreciate that. I'm going to get better. I promise."

Sanders smiled. "I know you will. You are stronger than you know. Hang in there and keep me posted on what is going on especially if you have to miss any work."

Faith stood to leave. "I will. Thank you so much for understanding. You have no idea how much that means to me."

She left Sanders' office feeling a little flicker of hope. Maybe Tina found a doctor that could see her and help her with whatever was going on with her. Faith finished the rest of the school day with a little bit of comfort. Maybe she was going to be okay.

After dropping the kids off at home, Faith went to the club to meet Tina. When she pulled into the parking lot she felt safe. No harm would come to her here. This place was her safe space. It was where she could run to in times of trouble and she was definitely in trouble. Tina's SUV was parked at the front of the lot. Faith pulled in next to her. Tina began to walk toward Faith as she exited her car.

"How are you doing?" Tina hugged Faith.

"I'm okay. Were you able to find a doctor?"

"I couldn't get you in for a month. I told them you needed help now. They told me to take you to the nearest hospital."

Faith's little flame of hope flickered out. "I can't go to the hospital. What could they do for me?"

Tina and Faith walked up to the porch and lit their cigarettes. Tina eyed Faith. "You don't have a choice. You're suicidal. You've lost hope. You need to take some time out and get things sorted out in your brain. You're no good to anyone in this condition."

Faith shook her head as she blew out white smoke. "Matt will not approve. He will never go for this."

"Have you told him how bad it is? Have you told him that you have thoughts of killing yourself?"

"No. He wouldn't understand."

"Have you given him the chance to understand? Call him and tell him that I am taking you to the hospital because you are suicidal. Now."

Faith had no desire to have that conversation with Matt. She had even less desire to go to the hospital because of her thoughts. *Do I really need a hospital? What could they even do for me? Am I crazy? Maybe I'm crazy. God, help me.*

Faith texted Matt what she was about to do. As she suspected he would, he called her while Tina was driving her to the hospital. Begrudgingly, Faith answered the phone. "Hello?"

"What's going on? What do you mean you don't want to live anymore? Talk to me." His tone was panicked. His voice shook with concern. He reminded Faith of a medic trying desperately to find out what's wrong with the patient before he dies on his watch.

"I have no joy, no hope, no will to live. All I want to do is lay in bed. I have no desire to do anything."

"Why didn't you tell me this before now? Why did you let it get to this point?"

Faith felt acid fill her stomach burning the edges of its lining. "I didn't let it get to this point. It just happened and has been happening for three weeks. I didn't tell you because I didn't think you would understand."

"You're right I don't understand, but that doesn't mean I can't help you."

"Well, you can help me now by just supporting me right now. I'm going to the hospital to see what they say. I'll see you later tonight. You know how long things take in the ER."

"Okay, I love you."

"Okay, I'll see you later." Faith hung up the phone grateful that he decided to be helpful. She had expected him to scold her as he often did. In fact, when she sat back and thought about their marriage he spent a lot of time scolding her, or 'correcting' her behavior. Quite frankly, she was rather tired of him trying to be her father instead of her partner. Yet, if she was being honest with herself she had been acting like a child for all the years of their marriage. Didn't matter right now, however.

As they pulled into the parking lot of the hospital, Faith wanted to tell Tina to turn the car around and go home. Fear overwhelmed her. Tina parked the car. "Let's go."

The automatic doors slid open revealing a room filled with miserable people begging for relief from their different ailments. *Great. This is going to take forever.*

Faith followed Tina up to the nurse's station. Tina held nothing back. "My friend is suicidal and needs to see someone."

Faith cast her eyes down. She couldn't look the woman in the scrubs in the eyes. She didn't want to see the judgement. The short nurse looked at Faith. "Is that true?"

Half whispering, half crying Faith moved her lips. "Yes, yes it is."

The nurse went to grab the phone in front of her. "I need to make a phone call. Can you please have a seat in the waiting room. We will get to you shortly."

Tina grabbed Faith's hand and guided her to the only black chairs available. "Okay, thank you."

Faith slumped down in the chair watching the people in the room. *I wish I were them. All they need is a medicine and they can go about their day. What can be done for me? Nothing. There is no cure for wanting to die except to just die. I should have jumped off that bridge this morning. Then it would be done. I wouldn't have to claw at my mind to try to keep it together. I wouldn't have to look at the stranger in the mirror mocking my every move. I wouldn't have to be a disappointment to everyone around me. I'm better off dead.*

"Get out of your head. It's killing you." Tina tapped Faith's hand.

"Then I'm screwed 'cause I can't exactly get away from my own brain."

"No, but you can stop giving the bad thoughts power. Stop letting those thoughts run rampant. Fight them."

A tear gathered in the corner of her eye. "How? How do I fight something I can't see coming."

"Faith Smith?" A nurse in blue scrubs holding a clip board called out.

Faith stood up with Tina right next to her. "That's me."

The nurse smiled. "Follow me please."

They walked through double doors that led into the ER that held beds filled with sick people. Several turns later they stood at a room with nothing but a bed and a T.V locked behind plastic screen. The nurse grabbed some pale blue scrubs from the shelf on the wall outside the room. "Here, I'm going to need you to put these on after I ask you a few questions and gather your things."

Faith's heart began to pound. Why did she need to put on

scrubs? Why were they taking her things away? What were they going to do with her? She looked over to Tina pleading with her to help. Tina put down her purse on the bed and walked over to Faith. "It's going to be okay. Just do what the nurse asks you to do. They are here to help you."

The nurse motioned for Faith's purse and handed her a plastic Ziplock bag. "Put her jewelry in here. I will make an inventory of what you put in. Don't worry we will make sure your stuff goes with you."

Go with me? Where the hell am I going? What did I get myself into?

This is what happens when you reach out for help. You get to go to an empty room and get asked to strip down and hand over your stuff.

I should have just jumped.

Faith handed over her stuff to the nurse who motioned for her to sit down on the bed. "I'm going to ask you a few questions and I want you to answer them honestly."

"Okay."

"Are you having suicidal thoughts?"

I have to say it again. Why don't I just post it on a damn bulletin board near the highway? "Yes."

She made notes on a paper Faith couldn't see. "Do you have a plan to commit suicide?"

"I made a plan to jump off the bridge after I realized that slitting my wrists probably wouldn't work and would be too messy." *I probably shouldn't have said that. It sounds crazy. It's the truth though. What the hell is she writing? Probably saying that I've done lost my mind come lock me away.*

The nurse continued asking questions. Faith's answers made her sound like she had already jumped off the bridge and landed in a dimension that only the crazy could fully understand.

Finally, the nurse was done asking questions. "Put on these

scrubs and just relax in the bed. A doctor will be by to check on you in a little while. Oh, you will need to take everything off including your bra and underwear."

Faith looked over at Tina. "Seriously?"

"Just do what she said. It's going to be okay."

Faith did as she was told. As she stripped away her clothes she felt pieces of her mind falling away. Tears pooled in her eyes. *What am I doing here? Could I have just gotten over whatever is screwing with me? Could I have just kept going? Why do I have to be here?*

She pulled on the paper scrubs that were so thin they barely offered a covering of her body. The cold hospital air pimpled her flesh. She sat on the bed with her knees pulled to her chest. The pools in her eyes burst and the tears streamed down her cheeks. Tina wrapped her arms around Faith. "You're going to get through this. It's going to be okay. One day you will be able to use this to help someone else, just keep going."

Faith sat on her bed watching the nurse who never left the front of her room. Every once in a while the nurse looked at Faith and smiled. Faith always smiled back. *Maybe if I smile they will let me go home soon.*

"Let me out of here before I kill someone!!!" Faith jumped at the man's voice that echoed through the room. There was banging on the walls. It sounded like he was throwing himself into the wall. A code was called. Men in scrubs rushed down the hall and into the room next to Faith. The nurse moved her computer back to the wall of the nurse's station and walked into the room where the man was shouting. Muffled voices. More banging. More codes. Now people in white coats rushed into the room with the angry man.

What part of the damn hospital am I in? Am I in psych ward? Holy crap that's where I am. "Tina! Am I in the psych ward?"

"Don't worry about it. It's just precaution because you had a plan to kill yourself."

"Don't stick that in me! I don't need it." The man next door kept shouting.

Well, I have finally arrived in life. I'm at the psych ward next to a crazy man throwing himself against walls. Never saw this coming.

A phone rang in the background. Faith couldn't help but answer it in her mind. *Hello, this is Faith I'm currently losing my mind, how may I help you? This is your life calling you do you care to continue the call. Not really. Like I said I'm busy going crazy. Try again later.*

A short haired woman in a white coat entered the room. "Mrs. Smith?"

Good. A doctor. Give me a prescription and send me home. I don't belong here. The guy next door does, but not me. Send me home. "Yes, that's me."

"Hello, I'm Dr. McBride. I'm going to ask you a few questions."

Here we go again. Faith answered more questions that were almost the exact ones the nurse asked. The doctor excused herself from the room and got on the phone.

Who is she talking to? Why won't she just let me go home? Oh, why did I come here?

The doctor returned to the room. "I found you a bed at a place called Timberlane Pines. They will take good care of you while you sort things out."

Horrified shock beat Faith across the skull. "Wait what? Where is that? What is that?"

The doctor smiled calmly and sat on the edge of the bed. "It's a hospital that specializes in cases like yours. They will be able to help you to get through this difficult time. You will be there for a few days."

"But, I'll be okay. I can just go home."

The doctor shook her head. "I'm afraid that's not possible. You need immediate help. It's okay. We all need help sometimes. This hospital will help you. The ambulance is on its way to take you over there."

Wait, what? An ambulance? I don't need an ambulance to take me to the funny farm; 'cause that's where they are taking me right? That hospital specializes in crazy people. Holy crap.

Faith sat in stunned silence. Tina stood up from the chair she had brought in to sit on. "Don't worry. I'll get your car keys to Matt. I'll tell him that they are taking you to the hospital. Just give me his number."

Faith gave her his number. Two men pushing a gurney stopped in front of Faith's room. *They are here for me. They've come to take me away.*

"Mrs. Smith?"

Faith looked at Tina with tears streaming from her eyes. Tina wiped them away. "It's going to be okay. Just let those people help you."

Faith answered the EMTs. "Yes, I'm her."

"Can you get on the gurney?"

Her body wouldn't move. One of the EMT's gently nudged her forward. Slowly, Faith sat down on the gurney and allowed them to lock her in. They pushed her down another hall away from a waving Tina. Doors slid open unlocking the outside world. Rain poured down from heavy skies. The ambulance doors were open ready to receive Faith in all her glory.

They pushed her into the ambulance and shut the doors. Faith felt the van lurch forward and onto the street. She watched the world outside dash away from her. Raindrops gathered on the windows and glided down the surface leaving behind streaks of water.

High ho, high ho, it's off to the funny farm I go. Well, Faith you have finally leapt off the cliff and almost landed into a padded room.

Sure, it's not technically padded, but judging from the beautiful scrubs you're wearing it might as well be a padded room. Hell, who knows maybe they will lock you away and throw away the key.

She watched the cars going here and there. *I wonder if any of them are as screwed up as I am. Surely, they are. I'm just the one that got caught.* A black Mercedes pulled up behind the ambulance. *Well hello, Mr. Mercedes. My name is Faith and I'm off to the funny farm. How is your day going? Can't be any worse than mine.*

Faith laughed to herself. *I probably shouldn't be laughing sitting here by myself. They might really find me a padded room.*

She watched the endless supply of cars, trucks, and vans whiz by. Everyone going somewhere and high speeds. Lines of office buildings, warehouses, shopping centers, and restaurants flew by the window. *Sure as hell wish I was going to one of those places instead of a hospital.*

The ambulance slowed down and turned into a long driveway that led up to a one story building. *This must be it. This must be where they are going to leave me.*

They opened the van doors and pulled her out. They wheeled her into the building. A woman behind a glass wall asked for a name. The younger EMT answered, "Mrs. Smith."

While they were checking her in Faith sat on the gurney watching the people in the waiting room watching her. *Yes, I'm crazy. I have the ambulance ride to prove it. I think it's all a bit much, but apparently my opinion on matters is null and void at this point.*

"Mrs. Smith, can you get up?"

I'm more than capable of walking. It's my mind that's a little wonky, not my legs. "Yes, I can."

"Good, follow me." The woman behind the glass wall led Faith behind a brown door that led into another waiting room. *Terrific. Another waiting room filled with hard chairs and pale blue walls littered with posters about mental health. Oh, good another plastic covered T.V. showing comedy shows that really aren't funny. Should be a great time.*

"Have a seat, someone will be with you in a few minutes."

Faith did as she was told. She hated waiting, especially since she had no clue what was going on. Someone did come out and take her picture. "This is just for our files."

Faith looked at the camera. *Oh, good I get to have a picture from the time I went to the funny farm. Great. I'm sure I look stunning in that photo.*

More time passed as she sat alone in the waiting room not really watching the TV. A young girl walked into the room crying and yelling at her mom that she didn't want to be there. *You and me both, sister. But, from what I can tell not all the shouting in the world is going to help you. In fact, I think it makes this whole thing a little worse. You should probably just smile and nod. Or, is it too late for that? I think it's too late for that. We're screwed.*

The girl and her mom were escorted down another hallway. Faith could hear the girl yelling at her mother about not needing to be here. A few minutes later the girl came back into the waiting room and plopped down in a chair with her arms folded across her chest. The mom tried to kiss her on the cheek, but the girl jerked away. *Can you blame her? You are leaving her at the funny farm against her will. I wouldn't let you kiss me either.*

The clock ticked-tocked on and the walls began to close in on Faith. Another woman entered the waiting room with a suitcase and sat down. *At least she has a suitcase. I don't have shit except these lovely scrubs.*

"Mrs. Smith."

"Yes."

"Follow me."

Faith followed the well-dressed woman down the hallway the girl had come from earlier. On each side were a series of rooms. One of the rooms Faith was instructed to enter into, and again wait for a nurse to come talk to her. So, Faith waited in a room with serene pictures of flowers hanging on the light purple walls. *Who are they kidding with these pictures and colors? I'm not at a hotel. I'm in lock-up cause my brain is screwy. I'm well aware of where I am.*

A tall fat nurse walked into the room with a file that Faith assumed had her name written all through it. She sat down across from Faith. "I'm going to ask you a few questions."

For the third time, Faith answered the same questions she had answered twice today. Except this time she cried. Maybe it was the way the nurse looked at her. Maybe it was the damn pictures on the wall exclaiming that she was not at some resort. Maybe she'd just had enough. Faith began to cry the kind of cry that required a box of tissues. Her shoulders shook up and down as she answered question after question with all of the honesty she had been running from. She had reached a point in her life in which running was no longer an option. She had to stop, to turn around, and to face the reality of everything.

"It's going to be okay. We are going to help you."

"People keep telling me that."

"Someone will be with you shortly to take you to your room."

A few minutes later a woman in pink scrubs came into the room. "Follow me."

Again, Faith followed another woman down another hallway. They passed through several locked doors before entering into the wing of the hospital that Faith would call home for the next several days. Clock on the wall said it was ten till eleven at night. Faith had been able to call no one. She barely knew where she was as she was traded off to another nurse who took her down another hallway and into a bare room.

Faith looked at the lifeless room with its naked walls and bolted down furniture. The walls that seemed to be closing in around her were painted a blueish grey. The color reminded her of a cloudy day that coated you with a fine mist. Frigid air circled around her making her feel the pain in her soul all the more. She took a deep breath and could smell a hint of bleach that always hung in hospitals. A thin mattress with a thin blanket waited for her. Someone already slept in the other bed. The nurse left Faith in her room sitting on the hard bed. She buried her face in her pillow and wept. *How did I get here? Why am I at a hospital? I want to go home. I want my kids.*

Sunlight peeked through the window in the room. Faith had no idea what time it was, but the person she shared the night with was gone. Faith threw back the thin blanket she had tried to get warm under all night. They kept the hospital unbelievably cold and her paper thin suicide scrubs were no match for the winter air that seemed to blow nonstop.

She got out of the hard bed and went to look through the small bucket of stuff they had given her the night before. There was a toothbrush, toothpaste, deodorant, shampoo and conditioner, and a comb. All of it was basic generic stuff that would barely get the job done.

Faith grabbed the toothbrush and toothpaste and headed for the bathroom. She looked in the warped plastic mirror. *No glass here otherwise one might break it and kill themselves.* She turned on the cold water and brushed her teeth. Her reflection was battered and broken. The eyes that once held life now reflected death. She put the comb through her tangled hair. Each pull of a knot sent tiny waves of pain that traveled from her head to her stomach. Tears pooled in her eyes, but she refused to release them. No amount of crying was going to change where she was.

She walked out of the room and into a hallway that led into a day room that had a TV locked behind a plastic shield, several chairs, and people that looked as broken down as she felt. Faith was tired, hungry, and thirsty, but there was no coffee, no juice, no nothing. Faith found a chair that was away from everyone else and sat there watching the nurses go back and forth. People stared at her—the newest patient to join them in this little break from reality.

A tall male nurse stood in the middle of the room. "Time for breakfast. Those with a green band line up to go to the cafeteria. The rest of you grab your tray."

Faith looked at her band. It was a red band. *Guess I don't get to leave this room.*

She followed the others with red bands to grab a tray. Faith opened the tray to find a hospital version of eggs and sausage. She ate the tasteless food because she was hungry. She really wanted coffee, but figured that was a luxury people like her couldn't have inside of this little prison.

She finished her breakfast and thought of her kids, of Matt. She needed to call them. She needed to hear their voices. She wondered if they were at work and school. Faith got up and asked the nurse at the desk if she could make a phone call. The nurse handed her a phone and showed her how to dial out.

The phone rang once. "Hello?"

Faith's body relaxed. "Matt?"

"Oh, my God. I've been so worried. We all have. We didn't know where they had taken you. The ER wouldn't tell us anything. Where are you? How are you?"

Faith broke down into a mess of tears. "They sent me to a Behavioral Hospital. Where that is I have no idea. I'm not good. I want to go home, but I don't think they are going to release me anytime soon. I'm scared."

"Don't worry. I'll call the hospital and see when I can come see you and what I can bring you. Okay?"

Sniffling, Faith wiped away the tears that wouldn't stop falling. "Okay."

"You just need to get better. It's going to be okay."

Her time was up. "I have to go."

"Okay. Hang in there. Don't worry about anything."

Faith hung up the phone and looked at around the room. *How will I get out of here? What are they going to make me do?*

"OH. My. God. You went to the mental hospital?" Carol was holding her full coffee cup. "But you were sober. How did you end up there?"

Faith noticed the sun trying to peak through the grey clouds. Its dance with the clouds reminded her of a little girl pretending to chase the stars while dancing in her white dress through the moonbeams. Once, when she was little, she had danced in the moonlight while on a camping trip. The scene outside brought back that wonderful memory. "When I quit drinking, I felt emotions for the first time in over twenty years. I felt every emotion that I had drank away. I had no coping skills. Add to the fact that my brain did not know how to function without the alcohol and I was a mess. I thought I had crashed and burned. I thought I reached my low, but as I've heard others say, 'my rock bottom had a basement.' I was to hit that basement with a force that nearly shattered my bones. And I would be sober the whole time. Let this be a lesson to you. You can be a drunk without the alcohol. If you don't change the way you act and think, you will come to know a hell so fierce that you firmly believe that God has abandoned you, but I digress."

"So, how long did you stay at the hospital? What did they say was wrong with you? What did Matt do?"

Faith paused for a moment. It was hard to look back on that hell. It was bad enough living through it, but revisiting those memories was painful. "I was there four days. They said I had major depressive disorder and put me on antidepressants that seemed to work but had a weird side effect on me. I was hyper and seemed to talk so fast I could barely keep up with what I was saying. I felt like I could take on the world and I had all of these ideas for teaching, for a home garden, for everything. I didn't know if I was coming, or going. All I knew was that I felt better and that I was able to see a light at the end of the tunnel.

Matt was wonderful during this time. He came to see me with tears in his eyes. He was so scared for me. I was scared for me, but I was able to lean on him during this difficult time. He brought me clothes for my stay and encouraged me. I remember when I saw his face, I felt a form of love that I hadn't felt in a long time.

"What about your job? Were they supportive?"

"To my surprise they were very supportive. Sanders wanted me to get better and was willing to give me the time I needed to make that happen. I thought my stay at the hospital was a turning point in my life. I thought when I left there I was a new woman who could take the world on and rise up from the ashes."

"I get the feeling that wasn't the case?"

Faith dug in her purse for her pack of cigarettes. She pulled out one of the cancer sticks and a lighter. "I'm going to go outside for a smoke."

"Good, I could use one myself." Carol followed Faith onto the patio that wrapped around the front of the coffee shop.

Faith lit her cigarette and blew out the smoke. "You're right. I wasn't a new woman. I was still a lost little girl stumbling over my feet. For every step forward, I fell back about four steps."

"What did you do?"

"Tore apart my family, ripped their hearts out, and stomped all over them. I was an F5 tornado that knew no boundaries."

CALL ME CRAZY

*G*lad to see you back. Was beginning to worry about you."

Faith looked up from the ground she was walking on to see a man she knew to be Paul smiling at her from the porch. She was attending her first meeting since being released from the hospital and was comforted to see the familiar faces. She hesitated to speak about where she had been, but in that moment she wanted to practice honesty. She wanted to stop pretending as she had been done for decades. "Yeah, I had a nice trip to the funny farm."

"Tina is looking for ya."

"Yeah, I figured she would be. She told me to meet her here as soon as I got home from the hospital. I'll find her."

Faith walked inside the building to look for Tina. She found her talking to a group of women. Faith hesitated to approach. She was afraid everyone knew about her recent stay at the hospital even though she knew that Tina wouldn't have told anyone. The fear of what people would think of her prevented her from going to Tina. So, she found a chair and sat down. Tina glanced her way and waved for her to come over.

Faith got up and walked over to the women she knew by face only.

Tina wrapped her arm around Faith's waist. "How are you?"

"Good, all things considered."

"I want you to get these ladies' phone numbers and I want you to actually call them everyday. You need to put yourself in the middle of the herd. Right now you are dancing on the outskirts."

One of the women laughed. "We go from living on the outskirts to being told we have to plop ourselves right in the middle of complete strangers. Hi, my name is Ruby. Give me your phone and I'll plug my number in."

Faith did as she was told. Each woman of the group introduced herself and gave Faith her number. Tina then pulled Faith aside. "We need to sit down and talk things through. If we don't get you on the right track you're going to go back out. When do you go back to work?"

Sanders had called Faith when she was released from the hospital. She offered her support and asked if Faith was ready to come back to the school. Faith had agreed to go back tomorrow because they were struggling with finding someone to replace her. Faith was nervous about having to face her students and the rest of the faculty after having left so abruptly, but she knew it was the next right thing to do. "I go back tomorrow."

"You sure that's a good idea? You have a lot of issues you need to deal with."

What kind of issues? Am I really that messed up? I did just get out of the hospital, so that's probably a pretty good indicator that I'm not all there. "I don't have a choice. I need to work. They need me."

Tina scowled. "You need to focus on your sobriety—and if you don't look at the issue that caused you to drink, you'll drink again."

Faith knew Tina was right, but she couldn't take more time off of work. Matt would never go for that either. "I know, but I can't take any more time off work. We will have to talk this weekend."

Tina furrowed her eyebrows. "Can you manage to stay out of trouble till then?"

Faith wasn't quite sure what Tina meant, but believed that she was okay. "Yeah, I can."

"You sure about that?"

"Not really, but what choice do I have? Besides, I'm feeling great. I have all of these ideas of things I want to do around the house and in my class. I feel so alive."

Concern dripped from Tina's voice. "I'm glad you feel so alive. I really am and maybe that means the meds are working, but what goes up must come down. You need to learn the tools to stop the crash you're driving into. Medicine won't help the issues that caused you to drink in the first place."

"Don't worry. I've got this."

Unconvinced, Tina continued. "I want you to call those women every day. I want you going to a meeting every day. I want you to stay focused on your sobriety. Make sure that you block out all day Saturday. We are going to use that day to really focus on the causes and conditions of why you drank."

"Okay."

"When do you go to see the doctor?"

"In a couple of weeks."

"Damn that's a long time. They couldn't get you in earlier?"

Faith was unsure why Tina was so concerned. She was on meds and felt fine. In fact, she felt better than fine. She felt on top of the world. "Since I'm a new patient, I have to wait."

Tina let out a sigh and ran her hand through her long dark hair. "Okay. Just make sure you do what I have said to do."

Flustered, Faith agreed. "I said I would and I will. I don't understand why you are so worried. I'm better now."

Tina's lips slightly turned up to reveal a smile of pity. "Honey, you are nowhere near better. You drank for 25 years. A few weeks of sobriety and some good antidepressants is not going to fix you. You have some demons to face, or you will drink again. I've seen it way too many times."

Faith moved to walk to her seat. "I'll be okay."

The meeting went on as usual. Faith was glad to be out of the hospital, but was now worried because Tina was worried. *What does she see that I don't? What does she mean causes and conditions? I drank 'cause I liked to drink, right?*

Oh, come on now, you know that isn't entirely true. You drank to hide.

Hide from what?

That is what you have to figure out. That is what Tina is trying to tell you.

Faith stayed a little after the meeting to talk with people she barely knew, but who made her feel like family. They offered her encouragement to keep going. On the drive home, she thought about Matt. He had been so supportive during her stay at the hospital. She felt bad for him being left to deal with everything at home, but he never complained. He just kept telling her to get better.

She was driving by a field of flowers that decorated the coastline of the bay she was driving over. *I want to run through the fields blooming with flowers. Red Hibiscus. Blue Bonnets. Purple Hydrangea. Flowers upon flowers. I want to dance in the sun until my legs collapse into mush.*

She pulled into the driveway to find Mary busting out of the front door to greet her. "Mommy!"

For the first time in a long time, Faith felt joy at seeing her daughter run to her. "Hey, baby. You ready for dinner?"

"Yeap, Dad already cooked it. It's spaghetti and garlic bread.

Are you going to eat with us this time?" Mary looked up at her with pleading eyes.

"Spaghetti sounds wonderful. I'd love to sit and eat with y'all."

"Woo-hoo!" Mary pulled Faith by the hand into the house. "Mom is going to eat dinner with us!"

Athena was setting the table. "Really?"

Faith went to help. "Yes, really. So, set me a plate."

Michael came running around the corner. "You're really gonna eat with us?"

Laughter escaped Faith. "Yes, yes I am. They made me eat dinners at the hospital, so I'm kinda used to eating dinner again."

Matt went to kiss Faith on the cheek. "Good to have you home."

Faith smiled. "Good to be home. Thanks for dinner. I really appreciate it."

"No problem. Let's eat."

The family sat down to eat. The kids talked about their day at school, Matt about his day at work, and Faith just listened. Listening was a struggle. So many things to do. So many ideas bouncing in her head. Yet, once in a while she was able to string together a few sentences from what each person was saying. It was enough to get by and she was proud of being able to listen at all to her family.

This is the first time I have actually sat down and listened to my family talk. Wow, what was I doing before?

Thinking about drinking, then actually drinking. Drinking was all you did.

Damn. I've wasted a lot of time.

When dinner was over the family worked together to clean up the mess. Faith went to take a shower. She was more than eager to wash away the smell of the hospital and to shave—they hadn't let her have a razor to shave without someone nearby to make sure she didn't cut herself. The hot water rushed over her body as she watched the hair and soap cascade down her legs and into the drain. *My life was going down the drain, but Tina says I'm not okay. I feel okay. Right? Am I not okay? I wonder what fragrance this shampoo is. They should have fragrances at the hospital. It's therapeutic. Maybe I should call the hospital and recommend it.*

"You okay in there?" Matt's voice broke Faith's concentration.

"Yeah, just enjoying a hot shower with good water pressure." The hospital had lukewarm water that barely spouted out of the shower head. "You okay?"

"I'm great. You going back to work tomorrow, right?"

"Yeah, I told Sanders I would be there. Oh, and Tina wants to see me all day Saturday to talk about why I drank, so that I don't go back to drinking."

A long silence passed. Faith turned off the shower. "Matt?"

"Yeah." His tone was harsh and abrupt. Faith knew he was gearing up for a fight.

"What's wrong?"

"Why do you have to spend so much time with her and with those people at your meetings. You are needed here. Your place is here."

Calmly, but with a side of frustration, Faith got out of the shower to dry off. "They are teaching me how to live without alcohol. You can't do that. Tina wants to get down the reasons why I drank, so that I don't do it again."

"I can do that. You don't need those people."

A side of anger was served up on Faith's plate that was already filled with frustration. She could feel that all-too-familiar rage fermenting just under the surface, but she didn't want to go there. She took a deep breath. "No, you can't. You are not an alcoholic. You don't understand."

His voice grew louder. "There is nothing to understand. You drink cause you want to get buzzed to take the edge off of the day. There is nothing wrong with that. You are not an alcoholic and I do not understand why you think you are?"

And there it was. Fury. It poured over her plate like gravy. "What is your deal? Why can't you understand that I'm an alcoholic? I just got out of the damn funny farm! Isn't that an indication that something isn't right?"

"You have depression. That's it. That doesn't make you an alcoholic."

Faith was putting on her pajamas. "Did you ever stop to think that I drank so much to avoid the depression? To avoid feeling?"

Matt followed her out of the bathroom. "You have happy pills now. How is that any different than you drinking? What!? Now you're just going to be a pill junky? You might as well drink."

Faith froze. The demon gleefully rattled inside. Rage simmered and stewed below the surface of her skin ready to ooze from her pores to drown Matt. "What the hell is wrong with you?! I might as well drink?! Maybe I should just quit my job and drink all day. Is that what you want me to do 'cause that is where I'm heading to if I don't learn how to stay sober?"

He raised his finger to her face. "You know what? You do whatever the hell you want to do. You always have. You should be at home with your family, but no go to your damn meetings and spend your weekends with Tina. I don't give a shit anymore!"

"Get your fucking finger out of my face. I have had it with you badgering me over everything I do, everywhere I go, and everyone I hang out with. I'm doing the best I can to be a better person and all you can do is bitch at me about drinking. My

God! I cannot actually believe you want me to drink. You want me to be a drunk!"

"All I know is that when you were drinking, you weren't moping around the house threatening to kill yourself. When you were drinking, you weren't so bitchy all of the time. When you were drinking, you were easier to be around. So yeah, I want you to drink again so you're not the crazy bitch you are now. My God you had to go to the hospital because you are so fucked up."

"Don't you go there you son of a bitch! I went to the hospital to get well, my brain doesn't have what it needs. That's what the pill is for. How dare you call me crazy! I'm not crazy. And you said I was crazy when I was drinking too. So which is it? Am I crazy drinking, or sober?"

He got in her face. Nose to nose. Mouth to mouth. "You're just fucking crazy. Nothing you do will make you better. You are never going to be right."

Tears welled up in her eyes. "Go to hell you bastard."

Athena shouted from the doorway. Her small frame shook with anger and fear. Her hands balled into fists as her arms hung by her sides. "Stop it! Just stop it! Y'all are both crazy. Just leave each other alone!"

Faith saw her daughter crumbling and knew that she was part of the reason. She saw a sad little girl trying to hold her parents together.

Faith glared at Matt. "Get out of my room."

He leaned over to whisper in her ear. "Go fuck yourself."

After Matt left her room, Faith called Tina. It was all she could think to do. Who else could she call? Lopez? No. Sanders? Hell no. Her parents? No, she wasn't on good terms with them thanks to the fights between them and Matt. So, Tina it was. She waited for Tina to answer the phone.

"What's up baby girl?" Tina's voice soothed Faith's seething anger.

"Matt and I had a nasty fight. He kept saying that I wasn't an alcoholic and that I didn't need the meetings. He also said that I was a crazy bitch."

"Okay, what was your part in the fight?"

"My part? I didn't start the fight."

"Did you do anything to stop it, or did you egg it on with your words? Did you pause and ask him why he felt the way he did?"

"No." Faith did not want to hear about her part in anything. Matt was in the wrong and that was that.

"Have you included him in your sobriety? Have you been open and honest with him about what you are experiencing?"

"No."

"Okay, so what you need to do is apologize for your part and start a conversation with him about your recovery so that he can feel included.

"Apologize! He started it. He called me crazy. He always does this to me. He always badgers me over everything. I can't take him anymore."

"Did you match his anger with your own anger?"

Faith grunted. She knew she had. "Yes."

"Then you owe him an apology. Period. You are responsible for what you do. You can't blame him every time you act out. Hold yourself accountable. Go apologize. Keep your side of the street clean."

"Fine." Faith hung up the phone and went to the living room where Matt was laying on the couch. No part of her wanted to apologize. But, she knew she was wrong for her reaction to him.

"I owe you an apology."

Matt blinked at her. Faith couldn't stand him in that moment. He sat there with a condescending look on his face and she knew that he saw no wrong in what he had said. She knew he wouldn't apologize. "I'm sorry for getting angry at you and saying what I did. I shouldn't have done that."

Matt continued to look at her. "I'm sorry for yelling, but you were acting crazy."

Every part of Faith wanted to slap him. "Okay. I'm going to bed."

She left him in the living room watching T.V. She laid in bed for several minutes thinking about his lack of apology, about how he never apologized because he never felt he did anything wrong. She wondered about many things, but there was one thing that kept bothering her. *Can I stay married to him? Could I survive on my own?*

The night was restless. She only slept for about four hours. The next morning, Faith got up to go to work. This morning she actually made breakfast for the kids. Athena was the first to the table. "Thank you, Mom. This is really nice."

"You're welcome, honey."

Athena ate a bite of the scrambled eggs. "Mom, why do you have to go to so many meetings? Why can't you stay with us like Dad wants?"

Faith sat down across from Athena while Mary and Michael filled their plates. "I need the meetings 'cause they are teaching me how to live without alcohol. How to deal with my feelings without being so angry all of the time."

"What about your faith? Doesn't God help you?"

"I believe God pointed me to these meetings 'cause he knew I couldn't do it on my own. I had tried to stop drinking before and couldn't do it. I don't know how, but I do know the meetings help. I'm trying to be a better version of myself. I'm doing it for you kids, so that I can be a better mom."

Michael sat down next to his mom. "As long as you get better I don't care how you do it. Just get better."

Faith grabbed his hand and squeezed it. "Thank you,

Michael. Thank you. Now all of y'all hurry up. As usual we are running behind. I need to get to work a little early, so I can figure out where I am in the lesson plans."

Matt didn't move from his bed. He didn't wake to say good morning, or to help with the kids. Nothing unusual, but Faith felt done. She was done with him and absolutely terrified over what that would mean for her and the kids. "Let's go." They left for school, leaving Matt to sleep away the early morning hours.

Sanders met Faith in the entrance way of the school. "Good morning. Glad to see you back. How are you feeling?"

Faith smiled at Sanders. "I'm good. And I'm glad to be back. Thank you again for being so supportive."

Sanders walked with Faith down the hall while the kids bounced towards the auditorium. "Like I said before, if there is anything I can do, let me know. I want to see you thrive."

"Thank you. That means a lot to me."

Sanders went towards her office. "Have a good day."

"Thanks. You too."

Faith went into her classroom. It was the same as when she left it. The substitute teacher had left notes on her desk. Each note told of what assignments the students did and what material they had covered. Faith groaned over the stack of papers she would have to grade.

"Good morning."

Faith looked up from her desk to see Mrs. Lopez standing at her door. "Good morning."

Lopez walked over to her desk. "When are you going to tell me what's going on?"

Faith sat back in her chair. She knew she had to be honest with Lopez. She owed her that for what she put her through with the HAC debacle and the Christmas fundraiser. "Have a seat." Faith motioned for Lopez to sit in one of the student's desks.

Lopez sat down and waited. "I'm an alcoholic and I have been struggling with depression. Last week I just kinda broke and needed time away to think about things and to get help with the depression."

She sat stunned for a minute. "Wow, I had no idea. Why didn't you tell me anything sooner?"

Faith shrugged her shoulders. "I don't know. I just thought I could manage on my own. I thought I had things under control. Turns out I didn't have control over crap."

"How is Matt handling all of this?"

Again Faith shrugged her shoulders. "Not very well. He doesn't think that I have a problem. He thinks he can help me not drink. It's not a very good situation."

"What about the kids? Are they doing okay?"

"Yeah, I think so. They just want me better."

Lopez stood to leave. "Well, I'm here if you need anything. Just let me know if you, or the kids need any help."

"Thank you, I appreciate that."

"Have a good day."

"You too."

Faith went through the rest of the day focused on her work. She felt energized for the first time in a long time. She was able to laugh with her students, to help them with their assignments, and to talk with her peers. She felt as if she had gotten through the worst of things. Maybe Matt was right, maybe she didn't need those meetings, or those people. Maybe she could do this sober thing on her own.

At the end of the school day, Faith went to pick up her kids. They were bustling with news from the day. All three seemed to talk at the same time. Faith wanted to take them for a treat. They pulled into a local fast food joint to get some ice cream. They each ordered their own ice creams and sat down to eat. Faith got up to use the restroom when another woman ran into her nearly knocking her over. Faith was annoyed but decided to let it go. Then the woman uttered words that would unlock the demon Faith thought was well under control. The heavyset woman looked at Faith with hate in her eyes. "Watch where you're going, bitch."

Tremors of anger shook through every limb. Her fists began to clench. Her jaw tightened. Her heart raced. "Excuse me?"

The woman turned to face Faith. "You heard me. I said watch where you're going, BITCH."

Faith didn't notice her children's pleading looks. She didn't hear Athena begging her to let it go. She didn't care that Mary was crying. Faith walked over to the woman and bent over her. "Fuck you, you fat ass piece of shit."

The woman slapped Faith across the face. "Mommy!" Mary cried out, but Faith didn't hear her. Faith was gone. She knew no justice except blood on the floor. She respected no law except survival of the fittest. She cared about nothing except revenge. Faith balled her hand into a fist, lifted up her arm, and landed her knuckles into the chubby face of the woman who was calling her a bitch.

Just like with the cousin, Faith pounded her fist into the woman over and over again. The woman's hands slapped at Faith, but Faith felt no pain. The woman hollered for her to stop, but Faith heard no voice. People tried to pull her off of the woman, but the demon inside yearned to see more blood pour out from the woman. Both of her balled hands beat down into the woman who was now laying on the floor in a pool of her own blood.

Sirens echoed in the background. Faith kept pounding. Someone said to stop. Faith kept pounding. A child screamed. Faith kept pounding. Suddenly, she felt an iron rod crash against her ribs. Shock waves of pain crashed over her crumpling her to the floor. A large man threw her down on the ground yanking her arms behind her. Faith kicked. Faith screamed. Faith felt her wrists being tied in chains.

"Mommy, please!" Mary hollered.

"Stop! Mom. Stop!" Athena screamed.

Faith couldn't move. The man on top of her had her pinned to the cold hard floor beneath her. "You are under arrest."

Slowly, the fog of fury lifted leaving Faith to deal with the aftermath. *Did he say I'm under arrest? What did I do? Oh my God! What did I do!?*

Faith turned her head towards the woman on the floor. Blood covered her face and the floor she was laying on. Bruises were beginning to show around both of her eyes. She was moving, but barely. *What have I done?*

Faith looked at her three children crying in the corner. Streams of tears poured down their cheeks. Their eyes were wide. Suddenly, Faith was pulled up to her feet. She could now see the cops that had wrestled her to the ground. She could see the cop cars waiting to take her away. She could see the ambulance ready to take the woman to the hospital. She could hear the cop telling her her rights. She looked at the man escorting her away to the back of his car. "What about my kids?"

"CPS will be here to take them to their father."

"Am I going to jail?"

"You nearly killed that woman. What do you think?"

Tears streamed down Faith's face. *What have I done? What have I done? Oh my God this is so bad. My kids. . .my poor babies. God, help me! Save me from this nightmare. I'll do anything. I'll do anything to get better. Please, just please help me.*

The car door slammed behind her. With every move her wrists ached. Her hands pulsated in pain. She could taste blood from the one punch the woman had managed to throw. Faith sat in the patrol car with her head down. Never did she predict that she would be on her way to jail. Never did she picture her future involving handcuffs, but here she was riding to her destination that would change the face of her future forever. Tina warned her that she had issues to deal with. Tina begged her to not rely on the medicine she was taking, to not do anything drastic until she took the steps needed to confront her demons. Tina was right all along. *What am I going to do? Dear God, what am I going to do? I hope that woman doesn't die. Oh please God don't let that woman die.*

The patrol car pulled into the police station. Faith was again yanked around and out of the car. The officer guided her through the station. Organized chaos hit Faith from all directions. Phones ringing, people chattering, computers glowing, and all Faith could do was follow the directions the officer gave her. "I need to call my husband."

The officer was taking her fingerprints. "You'll get your phone call in a few minutes."

Faith was placed inside of a small cell that possessed a toilet, a sink, and a hard bed to lay down on. The officer took off the handcuffs and slammed the door behind her. Her heart dropped at the sound of the door locking behind her. *Oh, my God. What have I done? What am I going to do? I will surely lose my job now. Matt is going to leave me. I'm going to lose the kids and for what? For some grumpy woman with a bad attitude. Why couldn't I have just walked away. Why did I have to fight? Why?*

Faith buried her head in her hands and balled till her eyes could produce no more tears. She got on her knees in the cell and placed her head on the floor. She was done. She was willing to do anything to make the insanity stop. *God, I give up. I give it all to you. I give you my will, my life. I beg you to help me through this.*

Faith lay curled up on the floor shaking and groaning. The void she thought was gone was back threatening to eat her alive. That all-too-familiar hell had returned. She was without hope. She was without joy. She was on the edge of losing everything.

"Smith."

Faith looked up at the officer standing in front of her. "Yes."

"You can make that phone call now."

Quickly, Faith got to her feet and extended out her arms so that the officer could handcuff her again. "My name is officer Gonzalez. I will be with you through this process."

Officer Gonzalez guided Faith to the phone. "Go ahead."

Faith dialed Matt's number with knots so tight in her stomach that she thought she might vomit right there. "Hello, Faith is that you?"

Her voice quivered. "Yes, it's me how did you know?"

"The caller-ID says 'City Police Department.' I have the kids. The Police and the CPS officer told me everything. Faith you are in a hell of a lot of trouble. I'm trying to figure out if I can post your bail, or if you are going to have to go to county jail."

"I can't stay the night in jail. I don't know what to do."

"You should have thought of that before you beat that woman."

"She hit me first."

"She is the one in the hospital. You do have that going for you that she started the fight. You could have claimed self-defense, but you went postal on her. I don't know if self-defense is even an option. I'm going to get a lawyer."

Tears came again. "How are we going to afford all of this? What about my job?"

"Consider that lost. You work at a Christian school and you just beat the hell outta someone. Do you really think they will be able to keep you on? I don't know how we will pay for this, but I will help you get through it."

Faith knew it wasn't the right time, but she couldn't help but to ask. "Are you going to leave me?"

A long silence passed. Each second made Faith feel more lost. Deep inside she knew the answer. "I don't know. I'm going to get you through this because you are the mother of my children, but I don't know if I can stay with you. I don't know who you are."

Officer Gonzalez signaled for her to wrap up her conversation. "I have to go."

"Okay, just hang in there. I will call Sanders and get with a lawyer, but expect to spend a night, or two in jail. I'm going to call your parents too."

Faith closed her eyes and sighed. She didn't want them to know, but she was in so deep over her head that she had little choice, but to let them know everything that was going on. She was probably going to need their help. "Okay, can you call Tina and let her know?"

"Yeah, I guess. You're gonna need all the help you can get. Give me her number."

Faith gave him her number and hung up the phone. There was no exchange of 'I love you.' Faith knew those feelings were gone. They had been gone a long time, but neither one of them wanted to admit that the marriage was dead. Now there was no going back. Faith knew that divorce was around the corner and all she could think about was how the hell she was going to survive? Hopefully, serious jail time was not in her future.

Gonzalez walked her back to her cell. "You will be transferred over to Harris County Jail and go from there."

So, that answered that question. She was spending the night in jail. Wow, had she hit the bottom of the barrel. "Do you know how the woman is doing that I hit?"

Gonzalez shook her head. "I don't know that hun. What happened to you? You don't strike me as the violent type."

Faith walked into her cell while the officer unhandcuffed

her. "I don't know. I seriously don't know. I just lost control. If I could take it back I would."

Several hours passed with Faith laying on the cold hard bed. She had bouts of crying mixed in with pleas to God to save her from the nightmare she found herself in. Most unnerving was that she could hear the shouts of the woman next to her claiming that she was going to fuck up anyone who entered the cell. That woman sounded crazy, dangerous. Faith didn't want to be in a jail filled with those types of people. *Honey, don't you think you are those kinda people? You did just beat the hell out of someone.*

Faith buried her head in her hands. *Dear God, help me.*

———————

"HOLY CRAP. What? How could you. . . ? I mean. . .I don't even know what to say." Carol was sitting on the edge of her seat, erect and focused. Her expression was a mix of shock and horror.

Faith sat in the oversized chair lost in memory. Looking back on the person she was was a painful experience, but one she was glad to be away from. "To this day, I still don't know what happened to me. Something inside of me snapped and all I knew was this rage that consumed me. It demanded that I act out, that I lay my hands of wrath on anyone who I felt deserved it."

Carol eased back into her chair. "So, what happened to that lady? Did you go to jail? How did you get through that? Did you stay sober?"

"About the only thing I did right was not drink. The lady had a broken nose and some major bruising, but nothing extreme— thank God. Otherwise, I may not be here sitting with you. I spent several nights in jail and let me tell you that was all I needed to set my ass straight. Nothing like being housed with a bunch of loose cannons to give you some perspective on how you should be living. Matt was able to bail me out and to get me a lawyer, but the damage was done. I remember that I kept thinking if I had just listened to Tina and not done anything drastic, I wouldn't be in the mess I was in."

"Why didn't you listen to her?"

Letting out a long sigh, Faith crossed her long legs. "After I left the hospital, I thought I was fine. Being on the medicine made me feel invincible. I thought if I just didn't drink, went to meetings, took my meds, and did my job I was going to be fine. I didn't realize that I never dealt with the 'why' of my drinking and that no amount of medicine would fix that. Everyone who is addicted to something has a reason behind it. Plus, as I would later find out, the meds were actually working against me."

Carol leaned forward eager to hear the answer to her question. "So, what was your reason for drinking?"

"That's not such an easy answer. It took a process of peeling back the layers I had used to cover the truth in order to find the root. I had to endure several eye-opening experiences to be able to see that root, and man were they some painful soul wrenching experiences."

Carol pulled her legs underneath her bottom and made herself comfortable in the chair. "I'm listening."

THE GREAT DIVIDE

*M*att was outside the Harris County Jail. Faith walked out of the double doors and into the sunlight she had feared she wouldn't feel as a free woman for a long time. The sun felt warm and comforting on her skin. She looked at her husband who stood with his arms crossed and an expression so stern she knew that whatever love he once had was gone. She didn't blame him. She had put him through struggles he didn't deserve.

She approached him. "Thank you for bailing me out and for finding the lawyer. She seems like she really knows what she is doing. She thinks I have a chance of serving probation since this was my first offense and because the woman did start the fight."

He unlocked the car and opened the passenger door for Faith. "I'm glad to hear that. I talked with Sanders. I told her everything. She wants to talk with you as soon as possible."

He shut the car door and walked around the SUV and climbed into the car. Faith watched him wondering who else he had told about her. She didn't want everyone knowing what she had done. "Who else did you tell?"

Matt started the car and pulled into oncoming traffic. "I told

Lopez. She asked about you, so I told her."

Horror struck Faith in her gut. "Why did you tell her? She will tell everyone at the school. She loves to gossip. Did you tell Martha too?"

"She asked, so I told her. If you can't deal with the consequences then you shouldn't have done it."

Faith sat stewing over what Matt had done. "I am dealing with the consequences. I just can't believe that you had to go and run your mouth to anyone that would listen. Great, now everyone is going to know what I did."

Matt glimpsed over at Faith. "You kidding me right now? You're gonna get pissy because I talked to people about what was going on? I needed someone to talk to. I needed help with getting the kids to school and home. I needed help getting them to soccer practice and their youth group at church. While you were in jail life was still going on. Don't have the nerve to get mad at me for needing someone to talk to and for asking for help."

Faith hung her head. She hated him for telling Lopez and Martha. He was always eager to talk about what she did wrong. He never talked about his part in anything. Maybe if he had been more supportive in her getting sober, she wouldn't have been so angry. Now she was going to have to face an entire school that would know her business. "I understand that you needed help, but you didn't have to go into details. Now everyone knows. How am I supposed to show my face?"

"That isn't my problem. Soon you won't be my problem anymore."

Faith turned to look at him in nervous shock. "What do you mean?"

He drove in silence for a few minutes. "I got a divorce lawyer. I filed for divorce yesterday. I'm suing you for primary custody of the kids. I have already arranged for me and the kids to live in an apartment. We are already moving out of the house. You'll be free to do whatever the hell it is you want to do."

That familiar rage fueled a fire from deep within Faith's soul. No one was going to take her kids away from her. No one. "How fucking dare you! You can't take my kids away from me."

Matt put up his hand to stop her from continuing. "Go to your parents and get yourself a lawyer. The kids are better off with me. I don't know who you are and I don't want to know. I don't care anymore. I'm done with you."

"You're done with me? Ha! I've been done with you for years. I'm not sad to see you go, but I have been a good mother and I will not let you take the kids from me. They are the reason I don't jump off a bridge."

Matt's voice raised. "You've been a good mother!? You're a damn drunk who is going to have to go to court for assault and battery. You are about to be out of a job. You have nothing. You are nothing. You will never amount to anything because you're sick. You're going to be one of those losers on disability because you can't handle life. I took care of you. I looked out for you. You won't make it on your own. You hear me? You won't make it."

Something inside of Faith broke. The last pieces of her soul shattered into a thousand shards. She wanted to jump from the highest bridge in town. If she didn't have her kids she had nothing to live for. Maybe Matt was right. Maybe she was a loser that would never amount to anything. Faith sat in silence the rest of the way home. The bridge loomed closer in her mind.

They pulled up to the house they once shared. Mary was the first to come running out of the house. "Mommy!"

Faith jumped out of the car to grab her baby and hold her close. She buried her face in her long brown hair and held onto her tightly. "Hey baby. I'm so sorry for everything."

Mary's tiny arms wrapped around her mother and her voice began to quiver. "It's okay, Mommy. No matter what happens I love you and I'm not leaving you. Daddy says we have to live somewhere else."

Tears ran down Mary's cheeks. Faith desperately tried to wipe them away. If only she could wipe away everything she had done. "It's okay, baby. You just need to know that no matter what I love you kids. I always have and I always will."

Michael and Athena had walked up to Mary and Faith. Matt stood with his arms folded in the background. Faith looked at her two older kids. "I'm so sorry. I'm sorry for everything."

Michael threw himself into his mother's arms. His voice shook with tears. "I love you and Daddy. I don't want to leave. Why are you doing this to us? Dad says you chose this."

Athena stood back unwilling to hold her mother. "Why have you been so selfish? Why couldn't you just keep doing what you were doing? Everything was fine when you were drinking? You're not an alcoholic. You didn't need those people; you needed us."

Faith rose to her feet and glared at Matt. "You sound just like your father. I am an alcoholic. If I had kept drinking things would have gotten worse."

"Worse than now!? How can you be so selfish? Now I have to leave and go live in an apartment!" Athena's eyes shimmered through the tears she was fighting to keep away.

Faith walked over to Athena and gently stroked her hair. "I have been selfish. I know I have, but please know that I love you and I am trying to get better for you."

Athena fell into her mother's arms crying. "You have a horrible way of showing it. I just want things back to normal. I don't want you and Dad to divorce. I don't want you to stop teaching at my school. I want you to be okay."

Faith swallowed a lump of tears mixed with anger. She got on her knees and held Athena in her arms. "You listen to me. I'm going to get better. One day I will stand strong and I will have you kids in my arms. Right now, I have to piece together my life. Right now, I have to learn how to walk again. I have to learn how to live. But, make no mistake, my love, I am not going anywhere. I'm not walking away from you."

Matt moved closer to the kids. "Tell her goodbye. We are leaving." He turned to Faith. "Don't forget about Sanders. She knows you got out today and wants to see you asap."

Faith's heart hurt with each pump of blood through her body as her kids hugged her goodbye. She stood in her front yard numb and unwilling to move as she watched her kids get into his car and pull away. They left her there to drown in her tears. Her phone buzzed in her back pocket. She reached to pull it out of her pocket and saw a text message from Sanders.

"I need to speak with you immediately. Can we talk now?"

Faith wiped away her tears. She just wanted to get this over with, so she could crawl into bed and cry herself to sleep. She texted Sanders back. "I'll be there in a few minutes."

Faith walked into her empty house. She couldn't break down now. No time. Her breakdown would have to wait. She went to the bathroom and looked in the mirror. That stranger was looking back questioning her. *When are you going to pull yourself together? When are you going to stop running?*

Faith splashed water over her face and brushed her hair. She wanted to take a shower, to wash away the smell of the prison, but she didn't want to keep Sanders waiting. She grabbed her purse and her car keys and made her way to the school. *God help me. Just help me get through this.*

Faith put the SUV in park and began to walk through the front doors of the school. She wanted to run and to hide, but she knew she had to face and endure what was coming. She walked into the front office and was greeted by the secretary Martha who looked at her with accusing eyes. Faith went to speak, but was quickly stopped.

"I know why you are here. Sanders is waiting for you in her office." Gone were the usual smiles and greetings. No jokes were exchanged just a cold and hard expression of condemnation.

Faith left the office with her head held down. She walked down a hallway she suspected she would never walk down again as a teacher. She walked by Mrs. Lopez's room and peeked in the window to see her standing at the front of the room teaching. *My teaching days are gone.*

She knocked on Sanders' door. "Come in."

Faith crossed the threshold of the door and waited for Sanders to acknowledge her. Sanders put down her pen she had been writing with and looked up at Faith. "I've been expecting you. Have a seat."

Faith cautiously sat down and waited for Sanders to lay down the punishment. Sanders' face was stern and unforgiving. "You were arrested for assault and battery. With that arrest you left me no choice but to contact the main office and tell them the current situation. Considering that your job performance has been poor in recent months coupled with your arrest, I'm going to ask you to resign from your position here at the school. I'm not firing you because I don't want that to be on your job history, but I cannot in good faith have you working for me anymore. You're not reliable. You need serious help to confront your issues and I hope that you get the help you need."

Faith hung her head and let the tears fall down her cheeks and onto her hands that were folded in her lap. She had not bothered praying because she knew that God was punishing her for her failures. What good was prayer going to do for her now. Afterall, she had prayed so many times before this moment and look where those prayers got her...fired. Sure, she was resigning, but everyone knew that she was pushed into that resignation which is just a nice way of saying "You're fired."

Sanders pushed a paper across the desk. "I need you to sign

this. It's your letter of resignation. I went ahead and typed it up for you, so you didn't have to worry about getting that done. I figured you have enough to worry about with the arrest and the divorce."

Slightly shocked, Faith looked up at Sanders. "How did you know I was getting a divorce?"

"I've been in constant contact with Matt. He has been keeping me up to date with everything. He is doing what is best for the kids."

Faith nodded her head as she lifted the pen to sign the letter. "No, he is doing what he thinks will make him look good. He always has."

Sanders gave Faith a quizzical look. "How is divorce making him look good?"

Faith signed her name. "You pity him don't you? I bet you have gone out of your way to offer him aide. I'm also willing to bet that everyone here knows his sad story and are going out of their way to help him. He made sure everyone knew what a victim he is, so that he can destroy my reputation and get what he needs out of people. Make no mistake. He is not grateful to you, or to anyone who helps him. He will use you till he gets everything he needs and then he will move on from you without so much as a 'Thank you.'"

Sanders didn't reply. She just sat in thought. Faith looked at her for a few more seconds. *I should have told you everything. I should have come to you sooner, but I didn't and now I'm lost.*

Faith moved to stand. "Thank you for everything you have done for me over the years. I'm sorry it came to this, but I will get better. I will be better and stronger than I ever was before."

Sanders stood and walked around her desk to meet Faith in front of the door. "I want to see you get better. I do. I want the best for you." She gave Faith a hug and watched her leave her office for the final time.

Faith walked down the hallway towards the front doors lost in thought when she heard, "How could you do that to your kids?"

Faith turned around to face the front office entry way. Martha and Mrs. Lopez were standing there staring at her. Faith just stood there caught in a trap. "Excuse me?"

Martha stood behind the secretary's desk sorting through the stack of paperwork. She spoke again. "How could you do that to your kids? You ruined their lives. I hope you wind up alone. You don't deserve to be happy. I'm glad you're leaving."

Stunned Faith stood there feeling her stomach twist into knots of acid. "I made a mistake. Last time I checked none of you were perfect, so how can you stand there and judge me? You don't know my story, my struggle, or what I've been through. All you know is what my ex-husband has told you."

Martha stopped sorting the papers and crossed her arms. Her chin lifted up in defiance of Faith's words. Lopez rested her arm on the counter just above the desk glaring at Faith. Faith clutched onto her stuff to prevent from shaking.

"When did you come talk to me? When did you ask me if what was being said about me was true? Oh yeah, you didn't. You just believed what you wanted, so you can stand on your high horse and look down on people who don't live the way you think they should live."

Faith looked over at Lopez who had stepped away from the counter and moved closer to Martha behind the desk. The two women stood together like a team against their opponent. "You're the biggest hypocrite of all. One time you told me about how God gave us community to help during difficult times. Well, you bailed on me. Did you ever once bother to contact me when I was in the hospital?"

Faith's voice grew louder. Lopez folded her hands together at her waist. She nervously glanced over at Martha and they exchanged smug looks then looked back at Faith who continued to speak. "Did you reach out your hand to me when I got out? Did you think to ask me about what happened when I got arrested? No, you didn't. When I was at my lowest and darkest point you didn't come to me to ask me what was going on. You went behind my back and listened to the gossip and lies my ex was saying."

Faith took a step closer to stare down Lopez for the final time. Lopez stepped back, her eyes widening with fear. Martha uncrossed her hands and took a step forward toward Faith, her chin lifting higher. Faith continued. "I struggled so hard to please you, but nothing I ever did met your expectations. Your community, your helping hand is only for those whose sins are tolerable to your disposition, or who have 'repented' and promise to live according to your principles. Everything you do is for your own glory. You need people to pat you on the back and tell you how great you are. Well, you aren't great. You're a liar. I don't need, nor want your community. Have a great life. I hope and pray that life doesn't one day knock you on your ass leaving you a shell of your former self cause you. . .you won't make it."

Faith turned away from them and started to walk out the doors leaving Martha and Lopez standing in shocked silence. *I'm done pretending to be someone I'm not. I'm done walking around trying to please everyone while I'm dying inside. But, how do I stop being so crazy? Tina. I need to call Tina.*

Faith called Tina on her way to her car. "Hey there. I was wondering when you were gonna call."

Faith unlocked her car and got in the driver's seat. "I'm ready. I can't live like this anymore. I'm ready to do whatever you tell me to do."

"What happened?"

"I'll tell you all about it when I see you. When can I see you?"

"Now. Bring your ass to my house."

"On my way."

Faith drove to Tina's house thinking about the past several months of her life. *I thought when I quit drinking everything would be better. It's not better; it's worse. How did my life get to this point? How did I get so screwed up? The only thing right I've done is not drink.*

She pulled into Tina's driveway that led up to a beautiful brick two-story home. The house was new and huge. Faith could see the edges of a pool through the bright new fence that surrounded a large backyard. Tina sat in her large two car garage smoking a cigarette. *Tina has a wonderful life. Why can't I have that? Why am I in this mess?*

Faith got out of the car and walked into Tina's garage. Tina blew out the smoke from her cigarette. "Tell me everything."

Faith sat down on one of the lawn chairs Tina had set up. She pulled out her own cigarette and lit it. She sat back as she exhaled the smoke and began to tell Tina everything about the arrest, the divorce, the loss of her job, and what she said to the people at the school. Tina listened attentively occasionally shaking her head in disapproval and grimacing when Faith described the fight. Finally, Faith was done. Tina sat silent for a few minutes. Faith expected her to bail on her just like her friends at school had done.

Tina looked Faith in the eyes. "How did all of that work out for ya?"

"What do you mean? It didn't work out at all. My life is a disaster."

"Yes, yes it is. Question is what are ya going to do about it?"

Confused Faith went to light another cigarette. "I have no clue that's why I came to you. I don't know what to do anymore. I'm lost."

"Have you bothered to pray about any of this?"

Faith rolled her eyes. "Pray? Yeah I've prayed and look where that's got me."

Unphased, Tina continued. "So, you're just a victim in all of this?"

Faith shifted in her seat. "Well, no, not exactly. I did those things, but—"

"There is no but. You either did, or didn't do those things. God had nothing to do with your actions. Did you do them?"

"Yes, I did them."

"Okay, so now you need to pray over the solutions to these problems you have."

"That's what I'm trying to tell you. Prayer doesn't work. I've been praying for years and this is the end result of all of those prayers. Disaster."

Tina's eyes widened. Her concentrated expression eased into a soft inviting smile. "Who is your God?"

The question hung in the mind trapped in a web of ideals that no longer made sense. A certain revelation began to rise over the hazy horizon. "I don't know." Faith fidgeted with her fingers while trying to release that final breath of defeat. "Once upon a time I thought I knew. I thought I knew much about everything."

Tina eased back into her chair. "And now?"

"Now? Now, I know nothing about almost everything, but I know God."

A smirk broke through Tina's porcelain face. "I see."

"What do you see?" Faith sat perplexed. "What are you seeing that I'm not?"

"You need to be able to start over. True spirituality is about the laying down of one's self in order to rise up in the arms of a power greater than yourself. So, who is your power? What characteristics do they possess?"

Movements of time and all of its trappings paused in a

frozen snapshot. Faith sat with her mind swirling. She nervously fidgeted with her fingers. Never before had she thought about who her God actually was. She had always just believed what other people said he was. *Who is God and what does it really mean to worship him? What does this power truly desire from his creations? What is the meaning of life if religion isn't there to cough up its often contradictory, if not hypocritical, explanations? Who do I want my God to be?*

Faith began to answer Tina's question. "They would be all loving."

"Of course. What else?"

"All powerful."

"Naturally. That's a good start."

Faith sat and sat. She didn't want to keep going. She really didn't understand what Tina was going for. What was the purpose of this exercise? Faith shifted again in her seat. She was growing uncomfortable.

Tina remained reclined in her chair. "Why do you hesitate when I ask you about who your God actually is?"

Faith longed to be somewhere else. "I don't know because..."

"Because why? What are you hiding from?"

Faith massaged her eyes. "I just want to go home. I'm tired. It hasn't been a good day at all."

"Of course you want to go home. You want to keep running like you have always done in your life. You don't want to look at God because you don't want to look at yourself."

Anger flared within Faith. "No! I look at myself too much. I see myself for what I am! I know me! I don't need to see more."

Undaunted Tina continued. "You aren't seeing all of yourself. What don't you want to see? Again, what are you hiding from?"

Faith shook in her chair half angry, half terrified. Tina kept pressing. "What are you holding back?"

Faith writhed her hands and grabbed her knees into her chest. "I don't want to do this."

Tina leaned forward and rubbed Faith's knee. "Face your fears; face what you feel. Stop running. Turn around and face what haunts you."

Standing, pacing, Faith's feelings welled up from the pit of her stomach. "I can't. I must. I don't want to."

An urgency broke Tina's voice. "Faith! Let it go!"

Faith pulled at her hair and bit her lip. A rush of adrenaline coursed through her body. She had to let it go. "I can't stand myself! Okay? I'm not worthy of love! I never have been." Tears flooded down her face.

Tina grabbed Faith by the shoulders. "Put down the bat! You are obsessed with what you should of, could of, would of done. You are human. You make mistakes. You said your God is all loving, right?"

Faith nodded her head yes.

"Then how can you hate what he loves and call yourself a follower of his?"

More tears streamed down Faith's face. "I can't help it. I hate myself."

Tina guided Faith back to her chair. She stroked Faith's hair while she thought over what Faith had said. "You need a new higher power."

Wiping away her tears with her hand, Faith looked up at Tina. She watched her go back to her chair and sit down. Her mind buzzed and swarmed with racing thoughts. "But, I have a higher power."

Looking straight into Faith's eyes, Tina's matter of fact tone hit Faith in the soul. "How is that working out for you?"

Faith snatched another cigarette up and went to light it. Her mind buzzed with a hundred different explanations. "I go to church. I teach religion to kids and adults. I know God."

Tina continued to stare right past Faith's defenses. "Again, how has that worked out for you?"

Faith shrugged her shoulders. She had no idea where Tina was going with her question. "I don't know."

"No, no, no. You do know. If you know your God so well then why are you here with me on the verge of a nervous breakdown?"

Faith paused for a moment, still unable to grasp what Tina was getting at. "I'm here 'cause I can't stop drinking and my life is a mess 'cause I keep screwing up."

"Exactly."

"I really don't understand what you're getting at, Tina."

Tina exhaled the cigarette smoke. "You got drunk with your God. You beat the shit out of a woman and went to jail with your God. Your marriage fell apart with your God. Obviously, something ain't right. You're missing something."

Faith wanted to jump to her own defense. She knew God. She debated atheists. She brought people to salvation. She did everything she was supposed to do. "But, I've studied many books, I go to church all of the time. I know God."

Tina shook her head. "You know of him, but you don't know him."

Such a simple statement. It's sometimes the most simple of ideas that are the ones that speak the loudest of all. Faith sat in stunned silence. It was true. She really didn't know God and if she were being honest with herself she didn't understand him at all. "So, now what? If I don't know him how do I get to know him?"

Tina put out her cigarette. "Start over and keep it simple. Come up with characteristics that you want your God to have and pray to that God. Just ask for help and give him thanks. He will let you know what you need to know as you go along."

Tina sat quietly for a few minutes watching Faith process

what she had said. Faith just sat in her chair completely defeated. Her legs were folded underneath her. Her arms were limp at her sides. Her eyes stared off into the distance seeing nothing in front of her. Faith now understood what Tina had been trying to get her to understand from the beginning. She knew nothing about everything, and, because she knew nothing, she was going to have to start over and figure out who God is, what life means, and who the hell she really was.

Tina broke the silence. "So, what is your next step?"

"I have no idea."

Tina got up from the chair and emptied the ashtray into the large trashcan that stood just outside the garage. "You go to the next meeting. You go home and eat dinner then call your kids. You give your God characteristics and then you pray to him. The last thing you will do today is go to bed and get some sleep. Tomorrow you start looking for a job. And remember that you may have to accept a minimum wage job till this legal matter of yours clears."

Faith got up to leave. Her head hung lower than it ever had before. She was spent. This day had beat her down into a pulp. She wanted to drown herself in alcohol, but knew that drinking would only complicate matters further. "Thanks, Tina. I'll see you at the meeting."

Faith got in her car and drove away. She watched as the landscape around her passed away in the rearview mirror. *Life is always passing away from us. The real problem is knowing where we are driving to.*

Faith watched Carol watch her. "I'd give anything to know what you're thinking."

Carol slightly smiled. "When I came in here today to meet

you, I thought my life was a disaster, but you, you were a mess. I mean how did you ever get through that?"

Faith laughed. "I warned you to not let my name fool you. I got through it one step at a time; one day at a time."

"That sounds so simple. That can't actually be how you managed to get through all of that?"

Faith longingly drank from her coffee cup. "Life is actually simple. The problem is that we complicate the hell out of it.

"Think about it. What do you actually need to live?"

Carol thought for a few moments. "Food and shelter."

"Good, I would say you need food, water, shelter, and love of some kind. Agreed?"

"Sure."

"Where we complicate things is in the actual getting of those things. We think we have to have certain kinds of food, shelter, and love. And those certain kinds have to be got in a certain way and what happens if those certain ways don't work and we don't get what we want? We throw a fit cause life ain't going our way. People are always going after the next level of the basic needs. They never actually stop and appreciate what they have right in front of them, and that is where all the mistakes are made."

Carol nodded in agreement. "I can see that, but you complicated the hell out of your life and you're telling me that your solution was one day at a time?"

"Yes, and I actually did what Tina told me to do cause left to myself I'll complicate cornflakes. Don't get me wrong I wasn't skipping through the tulips. My biggest hurdle was yet to come and it would be the hardest one to overcome."

"What could be bigger than possibly going to jail for assault and battery?"

"People. What people think of me was a big deal. Damn near lost myself in the thoughts of others."

A TIME TO JUMP

Faith laid in bed waiting for the alarm to go off. She didn't sleep well the night before. She kept replaying the day over and over again. She knew she had to get to a meeting and start looking for a job, but all she wanted to do was to stay in bed sulking. Finally, her alarm rang and she turned it off. She got out of bed and got dressed. She wasn't sure what she was getting ready for, but she knew she had to be ready for anything. Her phone beeped letting her know that she had received a text. She went to look and found that Sanders had texted her.

"Good morning. Can you come to the school after dismissal to clear out your stuff? We have a new teacher coming in next week and we need to have space for her material."

Damn that was fast. She wasted no time finding my replacement. She must have started looking the moment I got arrested. The last place Faith wanted to go was that school. Martha and Lopez would be there, and she didn't want to confront them again. She just wanted to be left alone to live her life the best way she knew how to at the moment.

Faith texted Sanders back. "I'll be there."

She went back to the restroom and looked at the familiar stranger standing in the mirror. They still looked lost and broken, but there was a small spark of hope in the eyes. Faith was clinging onto that small spark. *You can do this. Put your face on. Pray like your life depends upon it. Don't stop fighting. We deserve better. We deserve to be happy. Grab your life.*

Faith put on her makeup and got dressed. She made a decision to sell her house. It was a gift to her from her parents. Only her name was on the title, so for whatever she could sell it for the money would all be hers. Since, she couldn't afford to keep it and she needed a fresh start selling it was the best option. She was starting over. Can't start over in a house filled with the ghosts of a life now gone forever. She contacted a company that buys houses fast and made an appointment for them to come see the house that morning. *I can do this. I can survive on my own. I will prove Matt wrong.*

She started putting in job applications everywhere including grocery stores and warehouses. She wasn't afraid to work. She was afraid of not being able to pay her bills. She finally made the decision to call her parents and ask for their help. She picked up her phone and dialed her mom.

A calming voice answered the phone. "Hello?"

Faith sat down and began to fidget with her fingers. "Hey, Mom. How's it going?"

"It's going fine, but how are you? Matt told us you got arrested and that he was getting a divorce."

Faith's voice started to shake. Whenever she talked to her mom she felt her walls come down and that usually meant she was going to fall apart. Maybe she needed to fall apart, or maybe she had already fallen apart and was now just beginning to see it. "I'm not doing so great. He's taking the kids away from me and I lost my job. I don't know what to do."

"I knew he would do that. You just have to focus on getting yourself right. You need to find a job."

"That's not going to be easy. I'll have to take whatever I can get. I'm selling the house. I can't afford to live here anymore."

"You do what you have to do. What do you need help with?"

"I need a divorce lawyer, but I can't afford one right now. If I don't get one, then Matt is going to be able to take the kids away from me. He has ample proof that I'm not doing so great right now."

"So, you need us to get you a lawyer?"

Faith felt humiliated. She never wanted to involve her parents, but she was left with little choice. If she didn't get a lawyer, Matt would rake her over the burning coals and she may never see her kids again. "Yes, if you can manage that."

"Of course, I'll start looking for a lawyer. Don't worry about it. Everything is going to work out. Just give things time."

"Thank you, Mom. I love you."

"I love you too. I always have and always will. Don't forget that."

"I won't. Bye"

Faith hung up the phone relieved that she was going to have a lawyer and more relieved that her parents were supportive. For years Faith believed that they were disappointed in her, even angry with her, but now she began to believe that maybe she had just imagined those things. They had never said anything derogatory, or spiteful she had just assumed that they were disgusted with the woman she had become.

Now she just needed to find a job and pray that she didn't have to serve time in jail for her assault. She needed to call that lawyer. She dialed the number she had been given while she was still in jail. Faith tapped her fingers on her leg while she listened to the phone ring. Finally, someone answered. "McNair attorney at law, this is Jackie. How can I help you?"

"This is Faith Smith. My husband got Mrs. McNair to represent me and she came to see me while I was in jail. I was wondering what the next steps were."

"One moment please and I will transfer your call to her office."

"Thank you."

Faith tapped her fingers faster as she listened to the phone ring again. "Hello, this is McNair."

"Oh, yes. This is Faith Smith—"

"Yes, I remember you. You're the one that beat that woman and spent time in jail."

"Yes, I'm calling because I'm not sure what to do next."

"You have a court date in two months. We show up and I represent you. Based on what your husband told me I should be able to get you probation. We need to set up a time to meet and go over your case. When would be a good time?"

"Anytime, really."

"Great, I'm available this time next week."

"I can do that."

"Good, I'll see you then."

McNair hung up the phone leaving Faith to feel a sense of pride that she had accomplished several big things today. She was ready to go to the school and deal with anything Martha and Lopez could throw at her. She was strong, damn it.

Faith spent the rest of the day cleaning out the house of all the items she no longer used. Bag after bag of trash stacked up on the front lawn curb. Faith felt her burden lighten each time she dropped another trash bag on the curb.

The time on her phone told her it was dismissal at the school. Matt had arranged for his mom to pick up the kids, so Faith didn't have to worry about cleaning out her room in front of her babies. She grabbed some boxes and trash bags and left the house. She had no real intention of keeping very much. She had come to the conclusion that she didn't want to teach anymore and would not be looking for a teaching job. She wanted to start over and that meant what she did for a living as well.

She arrived in the parking lot and could see that Martha and Lopez were still there. She had hoped that they would have left by now, but knew that both would probably be there. All she could do now was hope that they would just leave her alone. She gathered up her things and went to the front door of the schools. Her negative feelings were still the same. A large part of her was relieved to be leaving the school. That place had become a dark corner of her life.

Martha was in the front office. She glared at Faith as she let her into the building. Faith didn't make eye contact, she just wanted to get to her room.

Martha saw her boxes and trash bags. "You cleaning out all of your crap?"

Faith looked at her and held back the anger that was beginning to boil beneath the surface of her skin. "Yes, I am. Hopefully it won't take me long."

Martha went back to her desk still glaring at Faith. "Good. The sooner you get out of here the better. You aren't wanted here."

Faith walked out of the office and headed toward her old classroom. *What is her deal with me? Yeah, I screwed up, but I don't deserve to be treated like I'm a piece of shit. I want to tell her off, but somehow I think that is exactly what I should not do.*

Lopez's room was open. Faith briefly thought about stopping in and saying hello, but then remembered the anger she had toward Lopez for not coming to her and asking her what was going on, for believing everything Matt had said, for abandoning her at her darkest hour. That friendship was over. Lopez made eye contact with Faith as she was passing by. She didn't smile. She didn't wave. She frowned and went back to what she was doing.

Faith walked into her room and stood there for a second. She had spent many hours in here teaching and laughing with her students. She was going to miss them the most. She had fought so hard to get them where they are now that she didn't want to just walk away from them, but that was the only option she had. She was being pushed out. Maybe it was for the better. Slowly, she started gathering up her books and putting them in trash bags.

She was lost in her errand and didn't notice how much time had passed, or that Martha had entered the room. "I see you're still not done. Seriously, how much of your crap did you have up here?"

Faith kept putting her favorite books in the last box she had. What Faith wanted to say and what she actually she said were two different realities. She didn't want any more trouble than she already had. "I'm almost done. I'll be out of here soon."

Martha walked over to Faith and stood face to face to her. The anger in Martha's eyes stroked the demon inside of Faith. She could feel the stirrings of a fight and was doing everything possible to not give into that demon. Martha took another step closer. She was so close that Faith could feel her breath on her face. Faith took a step back. Martha took another step forward. "You are a horrible person. I hope you go to jail. You hurt Matt and those kids. That is unforgivable."

Faith's hands started to tremble. "No, I'm not a horrible person. I made a mistake—"

Martha's expression hardened. "You're one giant mistake. Everything you do is a mistake. Hell, you wound up at the funny farm cause you're fucking crazy. Maybe you should go back and be locked up forever. Better yet, maybe you should do us all a favor and jump off the damn bridge like you were planning. No one wants you."

Shocked, Faith stood in place. The demon inside crumbled and fell into dust. Gone was her will to fight. She fought to find words, but only managed to mumble. "My kids..."

Martha stepped forward again. She was now so close that their chests were touching. "You're kids? Ha! They are better off without you. They don't need your crazy ass around. So, go jump. You're a loser and a bitch. The world doesn't need you. In fact, everyone would be better off without you in it."

Tears burned Faith's eyes. She didn't want to cry. The last thing she wanted to do was to give her tears to Martha, but the pain was so deep she couldn't hold back the tears. "I'm not a loser."

Martha laughed. "Oh, my God you are so stupid. You can't see that you are the biggest loser I know. You failed at your job, you failed at your marriage, you failed at being a mother. I've been more of a mother to those kids than you have. Go die, you dumb bitch."

Faith's body trembled as she scrambled to gather her stuff. *I'm not a dumb bitch am I? Maybe Martha is right. Maybe the kids are better off without me. Maybe I should jump off the bridge. I am a loser.*

Martha followed Faith around the room as Faith tried to gather her boxes to leave. Whatever was left could be trashed. Faith no longer cared, she just wanted out of there. "What's the matter? Nothing to say? I bet you want to hit me. Go ahead and hit me you crazy psycho."

Faith grabbed her purse and flung it over her shoulder. "Just leave me alone."

Martha paced around Faith as she tried to leave the room. "You're not welcome here."

Faith pushed past Martha. "My kids go here. I do belong here."

"Ha! Not if I can help it. I will make your life so miserable that you won't be able to show your face again. I'm going to tell everyone that will listen what you've done. Everyone will know what a psycho you are. You aren't going to have any friends by the time I'm done with you. I'll even get Sanders to turn against you. Just give me the time and I will whisper in their ear about what a piece of shit you are."

Faith walked down the stairs with tears in her eyes. *You can always jump off the bridge. Martha is right. You have no one. Besides, the kids are better off without you. Look at what you've done to them. Go to the bridge and jump. No more worries. Everyone will be happy.*

Quickly, Faith walked down the hall past Lopez's room and out the front doors. Tears were falling down her face as she opened her car door. The bridge seemed to be the only viable option left to her. She had let everyone down. She had nothing left. She was nothing. Matt had taken her only lifeline. Her kids were everything to her and now she didn't have them. They were better off without her. She had hurt them so deeply that only her death could bring them relief. She turned her car onto the street and headed for the bridge.

Martha's words kept repeating in her mind. *Martha is right. I'm no good to anyone.* Faith drove her car to the apex of the bridge and pulled over to the shoulder. She didn't bother with turning her hazard lights on. She opened her car door and felt the force of the cars speeding by. The wind blew through her hair. *Everyone will be better off without me. I can't live this life anymore. There is no hope of anything getting better.*

She walked around the front of the car and stood at the edge of the bridge, her hands wrapped around the beam separating her from the open air. She looked down at the water below and hoped that she would die of a heart attack before she hit the water. She hoped that it wouldn't hurt too badly.

The water below was a beautiful blue. *It's so pretty. I've always loved the water. Today I will drown in it and be forever asleep.*

The wind lifted her hair from her neck cooling the skin. Cars rushed by behind her. *Don't jump.*

I have no choice. The pain is too much. I can't keep going. All she could see and hear was Martha's words. How true they were. Faith raised her leg to crawl over the beam that stood before her and death.

I'm sorry God, but I can't do this anymore. I'm sorry I failed. Take care of my kids.

Faith's foot touched the tiny ledge on the other side of the beam. It was just large enough for her to balance herself long enough to get her other leg over.

"You don't want to do that."

His deep soothing voice, startled Faith. She looked over her shoulder to see a tall black cop looking at her with deep concern in his eyes. She felt a single tear slide down her cheek and fall onto her neck. "You don't understand. I can't do this anymore."

The cop took another step closer. "If you jump you can't change your mind. There is no going back once you jump."

"That's the point. I don't want to come back."

"You have kids?"

Faith bit her trembling lip. "Yes."

"What will they think when they find out you jumped to your death instead of being with them?"

"They're better off without me. They have their dad."

He took another small step forward. Faith could hear sirens in the distance. "They need their mom."

Faith shook her head. "I'm a mess. I screwed up."

"We all screw up. We can always come back from a screw up, but you can't come back from death."

"Everyone is better off without me. Someone told me that today and they're right."

Another step closer. An ambulance pulled in behind the cop car. Two more cop cars pulled up around Faith's SUV. The officer stepped closer. "No, they're wrong. Whoever said that was not a good person. Are you going to let a mean person take your life? Are you going to give them that much power?"

Faith's legs began to shake. She looked down at the water below. She wanted to fly to the water. She wanted that freedom. The cop moved another step closer. She stared at the water delicately moving with the current. "I just want it all to end."

The officer was in grabbing distance of Faith, but she didn't notice. Her focus was on the water below. She suddenly wanted to swim with the fishes, to let the water rush over her cleansing away all the filth that had gathered over her. The cop watched her carefully. "You can't let your skeletons become your kids' nightmares. If you jump that is exactly what you'll do."

Faith broke down crying. Her arms shook from holding onto the beam. Her legs ached at balancing over the beam. Her head swam with thoughts of jumping and ending it. Her memories were filled with Martha's and Matt's words. *Just jump. End it all.*

Faith went to move her other leg over the beam when she felt two strong arms surround her chest and yanked her over the side. The officer fell with her to the ground below. She felt his warmth and his strength as he held onto her so tightly she could barely breathe. "It's going to be okay. You'll see. It's going to be okay." He whispered in her ear.

Her body collapsed into sobs. She felt other hands pull her away from the officer and guide her onto a gurney. Tight bands wrapped around her arms and legs as the EMT's strapped her down to the gurney. She barely noticed that she was once again in an ambulance. She didn't care where they took her. She didn't care what they did to her. She didn't care anymore about anything. There was no hope, no joy. Life had become as dark as night and no lights were coming on.

———

"You were going to kill yourself? Why? Because of that Martha? And where did that cop come from? You were lucky he was there."

Faith looked down into her nearly empty coffee mug. "Words are power. I don't care what anyone says. What you say can either lift someone up, or tear them down and cast them into the pits of a hell so deep that not even a spec of hope can penetrate the flames. Her words struck my soul. I was already weak from dealing with my mistakes and from my mind slipping into a depression. I didn't have the ability to see any good anywhere. As far as the cop is concerned, I found out when he came to visit me at the hospital that he just happened to be driving not too far behind me that day and had a bad feeling when he saw me pull over. I guess you could say that God was looking out for me."

Carol studied Faith. "So, you went to the hospital again?"

"Yeah. This time they kept me a week. I finally did see my doctor that I had an appointment with before I went to the first hospital. She came to the hospital after I called her office to tell her why I couldn't make it to see her."

"That's an amazing doctor."

Faith put down her coffee. "Yeah, when she found out they had to pull me from the edge of the bridge she realized that I was in a pretty sad state of affairs. She helped save my life."

Carol crossed her legs and looked at Faith with a new understanding. "When I first came in here I thought you were just some feel good activist like I had come across before."

Faith sipped from her coffee mug waiting for Carol to

continue. "I had tried to get help before and the people always had good intentions, but their knowledge came from books; not experience. I was afraid that you were going to be the same way."

Faith smiled. "And now?"

Carol twirled her fingers around a strand of hair. "Now I can feel your story. So many parts were like my own. How you survived all of that might be able to help me. What exactly did the doctor do for you? Did she give you new meds?"

Leaning back in her chair, Faith looked out the floor-to-ceiling windows of the coffee shop. "She was able to hear me when no one else could."

NEW HOPE

The drive to the hospital went by in a blur. Faith felt numb all over. She was a zombie that could follow directions. She was checked into Tranquility Hospital and asked all the same questions as she was asked at the other hospital just weeks before. She answered them all through rounds of sobbing.

She followed a nurse in blue scrubs down a long hallway with windows looking onto a garden that held flowers and trees dancing in the wind. She went into an elevator and went up several stories before being led into another wing of the hospital. The nurse handed her off to another nurse in pink scrubs before leaving Faith standing in the middle of a day room that had brightly colored walls and large cushioned chairs. The room was warm and inviting. The hospital was completely different from the other one. There were happy colors on the wall and bright big windows looking out onto gardens. The atmosphere of the hospital was one that encouraged hope. The walls themselves seemed to invite you to leave the despair behind. The nurses even seemed happier than at the other hospital.

The nurse in pink scrubs gently placed her hand on Faith's shoulder. "Come over here to the table and I can get you set up in your room."

Faith sat down at the table. The nurse came over with a bucket. "The other patients are at dinner right now, but will be back shortly. Here is your bucket of soaps, a toothbrush, and some towels. You can take a shower if you want."

Faith took the stuff. "I need to call my parents."

"Of course. The phones are on the wall over there." She pointed to a wall behind Faith. "You can use them anytime during the day as long as there isn't a group session going on. We do ask that you limit your time so that everyone gets a chance to use the phones."

"Can I make a call now."

"Go ahead."

Faith picked up the phone and dialed her mom. "Hello?"

Faith started to cry again. "Mom?"

"Faith! Thank God. The police called me earlier and told me that you were going to jump off the bridge! Baby, why would you do that? Do you have any idea what that would have done to your dad and me? What about your kids?"

"Everything just seems so hopeless, Mom. I'm stuck in the dark and can't seem to find my way out."

"There is always hope. Even if there's only the smallest spec, there is hope. Where are you?"

"I'm at Tranquility Hospital. Can you bring me some clothes and cigarettes."

"Yes. I'll do anything to help. I'll bring the stuff by today. Will I be able to see you today?"

"I doubt that. They have me on lockdown until I see a doctor. Speaking of doctors I need to call mine. I have to go."

Faith's mom's voice rattled behind the tears she was holding back. "I love you. Please never forget that. I don't know what I would do without you. Please remember that."

"I'll try. I love you too."

Faith dialed the number of her doctor's office and told them where she was and why. When she hung up the phone the nurse was standing behind her. "My name is Samantha. If you need anything don't hesitate to ask. I've ordered you a dinner. It should be here shortly."

"Okay."

"Let me take you to your room."

Faith followed the nurse down a long hallway that had rooms on each side. The setting sun painted the hallway in golden light. "Here is your room. You're lucky. You don't have a roommate yet."

The room was the same as it was in the other hospital. The furniture was minimal and bolted down. The bed hard and the blankets sparse against the frigid bleach-tinged air. However, there was a window that allowed for the sunlight to pour into the room and cast dancing shadows on the pale blue walls. Faith put her bucket on the bed and got ready to take a shower.

The warm water fell over her. Faith tried to wash her hair, but her arms were too heavy. She coated her body with soap and let the water rinse her off. She stood there in the shower thinking of her kids. *My babies. I just want my babies. Why did they leave me?*

Faith sank down onto the bottom of the shower where she sat letting the water rain down over her. She wanted to move, but couldn't find the energy to do so. Many minutes passed, but for Faith time held no meaning.

"Faith? Are you alright?"

Nurse Samantha was calling Faith from the bedroom. Faith couldn't find the will to answer her.

"Faith?" Samantha had entered the bathroom. She moved

the curtain slightly to peek in on Faith. "Honey, you need to get up and get out of the shower."

Crying Faith buried her head in her knees. "I just want my babies."

"I know honey, but you have to get out of the shower. Your doctor is here to see you. Trust me that's a good thing. Once you see her you can go out to the dining hall and to smoke. Come on. Get up."

Samantha turned off the shower and handed Faith a towel. Faith grabbed Samantha's hand and pulled herself up to stand. She stood in the bathroom unphased by her own nudity in front of a stranger. "Faith, honey, you need to dry off and put your clothes back on. Can you do that?"

Faith nodded her head. She did want a cigarette, so she dressed herself after Samantha left and went out into the day room. Voices clamored around her. The other patients were back from dinner. Faith took little notice of them. Samantha greeted her. "Good for you. You got out of the shower and dressed. You should be proud. Follow me. Your doctor is through here."

Faith walked behind Samantha down another short hallway that led away from the bright day room and led into a small office. The bare office walls were painted a pale pink. No paintings hung on the wall. No decorations adorned the desk. It was just a room that served a single purpose; doctors diagnosing patients. A black woman with smooth, glowing skin sat behind the simple small desk. Her long hair curled just beneath her shoulders. Her purple pain suit framed her curvy figure. She looked up from the binder she had been thumbing through. "You must be Faith."

"Yeah."

"Have a seat. Thank you, Samantha. She'll be alright."

"I'm Dr. Stevens. When I heard why you were going to miss our appointment I came over here."

Dr. Stevens continued to thumb through the large binder filled with papers that Faith figured was all about her. "That's a big binder. I must be really screwed up."

Laughing at Faith's attempt to have humor, Dr. Stevens looked up from the binder. "You're not screwed up. You're just lost and I'm here to help you find your way. I see here that they have you on antidepressants. How did you feel when you started taking them?"

"I felt great. I had lots of ideas, plans. I felt like I could take on the world."

Dr. Stevens nodded. "Were you sleeping?"

"Now that you ask me that. No, I really wasn't. I would get about 4 hours of sleep."

"Did you notice if you were talking fast? Did you spend a bunch of money for no real reason?"

Faith was a little shocked by the questions because the answers were 'yes'. How did she know? "Yes, I did. I went and bought a bunch of stuff about knitting cause I wanted to start that as a hobby."

Dr. Stevens nodded her head. "It says in your file that you have 'Major Depressive Disorder.'"

"Yes."

"People with major depressive disorder don't do crazy things and lose sleep when they are on antidepressants."

"Do you have any family history of Bipolar Disorder in your family?"

Faith's eyes grew wide. "Yes, my grandmother." Faith's grandmother attempted suicide several times and exhibited some of the same behaviors that Faith had over the years, especially since she sobered up.

"I believe you have Bipolar 2 Disorder. I'm going to start you on some medicine that won't send you into a hypomanic state."

Faith sat in her chair very confused. "What is that and what is hypomanic? Isn't Bipolar Disorder a thing for crazy people?"

Dr. Stevens shifted in her chair. "Bipolar 2, and Bipolar in general, is a mood disorder with periods of hypomania and depression. Bipolar 1 disorder has mania and depression. Bipolar 2 has hypomania and depression. Hypomania is an elevated state of mood in which the patient can exhibit behaviors that go against the normal behavior of the patient. You can feel unusually hyper, irritable, have racing thoughts, increased self-esteem, and decreased need for sleep. You will do things you normally wouldn't do and buy things you normally wouldn't buy. It's a little different from the mania people with Bipolar 1 disorder have. Bipolar doesn't mean crazy. It means the person who has it can't control the swings between moods. They aren't crazy. They are trying to live with a brain chemistry imbalance that threatens their lives."

"So, I'm not crazy just sick? That hypomania doesn't sound so bad. It sounds better than where I'm at now."

The doctor's face stiffened. "It's actually quite serious. During hypomania you will engage in activities that are dangerous. It says here that you were arrested for assault and battery. I'm willing to bet you lost all semblance of control and had no idea why. That's a symptom of hypomania. More importantly what goes up must come down. After hypomania, there is the deep depression that follows. Usually, something will trigger a depressive episode. This is a deep depressive episode that you are in now. You will need medicine that keeps you at an even mood. And, no, you are not crazy."

For the first time since she stopped drinking, Faith had a glimmer of hope. If she were being honest, it was the first time in her life that she felt she had answers to the reasons behind why she had always felt depression with brief periods of feeling great. There was something wrong with her and there were medicines to help. She wasn't crazy; she was off balance. She had begun to believe that she was insane, but this diagnosis opened up the door to solutions that could help solve the way she felt. She looked at the doctor. "But, why am I like this?"

"We really don't know the 'why' of Bipolar. We think it's genetic in part. Just look at it this way. Your brain doesn't have the right levels of chemicals that everyone else does. That's not your fault. The best part is that if you take your medicine as prescribed then you should be able to live a fairly normal life. Sure, things will be harder for you than someone without Bipolar, but you can live and even thrive. It's just going to take time. We need to find the right medicine at the right dose and you will need some therapy to cope with your triggers. For years, you used alcohol to cope. Now you need to find healthy tools for coping with life. But, first things first. I'm going to prescribe you some medicine that you will start taking tonight."

"Okay, that sounds good."

"Just hang in there. Life will get better. You won't be in here forever and life out there has endless possibilities."

Faith looked down at her fingers. "I don't know if I believe that."

Dr. Stevens' eyes softened. "Then believe that I believe. It's a process and is going to take time. Give yourself time. Don't be impatient."

Faith let out a sigh of relief. "I'm not crazy?"

Dr. Stevens smiled. "Absolutely not. You're just a little off balance at the moment. In time, we will get you where you need to be. So, no jumping off of bridges okay?"

Faith gave a weak smile and nodded her head. "Okay." She left the office with a new sense of self. Now she had someone who believed in her. Someone who had given her a candle to light up the dark room she had been living in for so long.

"Faith?" Nurse Samantha called as Faith left the office.

"Yes?"

"You have a bag of stuff that your mom brought. You also get the green band to leave the day room with the others. See? Your day is getting brighter."

Faith took the brown paper grocery bag filled with clean clothes, pajamas, and left the several packs of cigarettes with the nurse. Faith smiled. She was going to hold onto that candle with every ounce of strength she still had.

It was 8 p.m. according to the wall clock and Faith noticed that some of the women she was in the unit with were getting antsy. She leaned over to a woman sitting next to her and asked, "What is going on?"

The short blonde haired woman smiled. "They're getting ready to go smoke. This is our last outside time of the day. You going out with us? I see you have a green band. That means you get to be a big girl and go outside."

Excited for a cigarette, Faith nodded her head quickly. "Yes, I am. Been wanting a cigarette all day."

"Then you're in luck. Outside time is smoke time. My name is Edith. What's your name?"

"Faith. Nice to meet ya. Wish we were someplace else."

"Ain't that the truth. What did you do to earn your spot here?"

"Tried to learn to fly off of a bridge. You?"

"My friend brought me in 'cause I wasn't doing well. I started cutting myself again." Edith showed Faith her arm. The cuts were still fairly fresh."

Faith cringed inside, but felt a bit of relief that someone else was like her. "I started cutting myself when I stopped drinking. It was the only way I could deal with the overwhelming pain. I kept that well-hidden."

"I understand completely, most people don't. They look at ya like you're crazy, but I'm just like, *if you could walk a mile in my shoes then you wouldn't be so judgey.*"

Nurse Samantha stood up from behind the desk. "Smoke break. If you're going outside come get your cigarettes."

Faith and Edith both stood up and walked to the desk. Each person got two cigarettes. They followed the nurse's aide to the outside area. The building looked so different in the nighttime. The windows acted as mirrors and reflected the women as they walked to the doors leading to the outside garden. Faith couldn't imagine a more pitiful sight that the reflection revealed. Here was a group of women, that society said was broken and needed repair, pushed together to try to figure out the 'why' of their predicaments.

Faith felt the warmth of the spring rush over her as the doors opened. The air outside was fresh and the slight breeze blew through their hair. Faith loved the feeling of a gentle wind lifting its fingers through her hair. She lit her cigarette and looked at the night sky. She couldn't see too many stars because they were in the city, but the few she could see glimmered from far away. She felt so small in comparison with the rest of the world.

"You like the night sky?" Edith had come to sit next to Faith.

"Yeah, reminds me of when I was a kid spending my summers in Colorado. The night sky there is beautiful."

"I bet. Don't get to see too many stars here. So, what did your doc say you have? I have major depressive disorder."

Faith hesitated for a minute. She was unsure about saying out loud what her disorder actually was. Saying it made it real. "Bipolar 2 disorder. Still not sure what exactly that means."

Edith nodded her head. "You should talk to some of the women in here. They have Bipolar too. You're not alone." She pointed to a brunette haired woman sitting several feet away. "That's Meredith. She has Bipolar. She was here when I got here. She's had a rough time of it."

Faith didn't want to talk to anyone about Bipolar. She really didn't want to talk to anyone about much of anything. She liked talking to Edith though. Edith had a great sense of humor despite her disorder trying to kill her. "I don't know. Maybe."

The nurse stood up. "Time to go back in. Everyone line up."

Faith and Edith did as they were told. The group of women followed the nurse back into the building. Faith leaned over to Edith. "What's next?"

Edith looked up at Faith. "We have about an hour and a half before we have to go to bed. Lights out at 10. You can watch T.V., or go to bed."

"Going to bed sounds nice. I'm drained."

"Being suicidal will do that to ya. You still feel like you want to jump from the bridge?"

Faith paused while the group waited for the door to their wing of the hospital was unlocked. Everyone filed into the day room to watch T.V. or to talk. Edith sat down in one of the over-sized chairs. Faith sat next to her. "I don't know. I still feel hopeless. I still want to die, but I have a tiny seed of hope. I guess. . .I really don't know much about anything to be honest. I do know that I'm miserable."

Edith laughed. "Hey, that's a good start. When you don't know much about anything it means you're ready for anything to happen. It's not so bad not knowing anything. I don't know much about anything myself."

Perplexed, Faith crossed her legs in the chair. "If not knowing anything is so great then how did you wind up here at the funny farm?"

"Not knowing anything about anything has given me wisdom. I know that sounds crazy, but hear me out. When you don't know much you can finally learn about everything you need to learn in order to function. No offense, but I'm not here 'cause I was about to jump off the bridge. I'm here 'cause I know my meds stopped working and I needed some extra help while they fixed my med situation. I had the wisdom to know it was time for help. Keep at it and you will know when it's time for help before you become so desperate that you want to die."

"I think I get it. Maybe one day I'll be able to be more like you."

Edith violently shook her head. "No, no, no. Not like me. You need to grow into yourself. You need to become more like you— the you you lost along the way in life. Keep fighting and you will find your lost self. Just takes time."

"You're right. Thank you. I really needed to hear that. I'm going to go to bed now."

"Right behind ya. They wake you up early for breakfast. Good night."

Faith rose to walk to her room. "Good night."

She walked into her room and crawled into bed. She layed there thinking about how the day went and how she once again wound up in the hospital. Why did she let Martha get to her so deeply? Why did she let Matt's words pierce her soul and torment her? Why did she care so much about what people thought of her? These were the questions that haunted her. She needed to talk to Tina about them. She needed to rid herself of the bondage of societal norms and standards. Afterall, she had spent her entire life following those norms and standards and what did it get her? Misery. Nothing, but misery. Faith fell asleep wondering how to free herself from a world that was hell bent on making her conform.

"I'LL BE DAMNED. You have bipolar? Damn woman was there anything that was going right with you? I mean your life was like a damn soap opera."

Faith laughed. "Yes, it was. But, ya know going to the hospital was the best thing for me. Each day I was there I could feel myself getting stronger and stronger. I went to all of the groups and learned that I had to forgive myself and others who had wronged me. The hardest person to forgive is the self."

"Why is that? I would think forgiving those who have wronged you would be harder."

"Don't get me wrong. Forgiving others is difficult, especially when they feel they have done nothing wrong. However, forgiving the self is hardest cause you get consumed with what other people think of you. You compare your insides to the outsides of other people. You constantly think that you should have done this, or could have done that, but the truth is that you are human and make mistakes. Some people won't let you forget those mistakes, but they are sick people with nothing better to do than to go around trying to make themselves feel better about their lives."

Carol shifted in her seat. "What about Edith? She seems like a wise person."

"Oh, I value her to this day. We still talk and get together when we can. I value her friendship. She has helped me get through some dark times."

Carol's expression hardened. "Something is bothering me about what you said. You mentioned that you were a slave to society or something like that. What do you mean?"

Faith put down her coffee mug on the table in front of them and leaned back in her chair crossing her legs at the ankles. "When you sit back and think about it we are all slaves to society in one form or another. From the time you're born your parents, teachers, and government tell you what is good and what is bad.

You're told what should make you happy and what will make you unhappy. You have no real say in how to mold your life because you make decisions based on what everyone else tells you to do. You don't truly follow what makes you. the individual, happy. You follow what society says is best for you based on its need for you to conform and be another member of the collective."

"Whoa there, that's a little much don't ya think? I mean really." Carol leaned back in her chair and crossed her legs. Her face revealed a bit of cynicism.

Faith shrugged her shoulders. "When was the last time you made a decision based on what you truly wanted for yourself without factoring in what other people would think?"

Carol sat in silence for several minutes. "I. . .I really haven't."

"There ya go."

Carol gently shook her head. "Anyway, so, what did you do when you got out of the hospital?" Carol gazed at Faith.

"The first thing I did was call Tina. I knew I had to deal with my demons before they crept up on me again and I found myself in more trouble. People with addiction don't get to run from demons. They either fight them, or die."

BREAKING DAWN

*T*oday's the big day. You get to go home. You excited?"
Nurse Samantha was handing Faith papers to sign
before she was discharged.

"Yes, I am, but I'm scared too. I have a lot to deal with."

Samantha nodded her head. "Just remember to deal with
one thing at a time. And to keep your appointments with your
doctor. Your life depends on it."

Faith smiled. "I know and I'm actually going to try something different this time like reaching out to others and talking
through issues."

"Good for you. Just don't give up. Your babies need you."

The phone rang and Samantha answered it. "Hello? Oh,
okay. Thank you."

Samantha smiled and looked at Faith. "Your ride is here. It's
time for you to go."

Faith's limbs shook. Her stomach flipped inside of her. She
was ready to get out of the hospital and to deal with the mess
that was her life. Faith followed Samantha out of the day room
and into the hallway. Each step toward the exit doors felt like a

step towards her life. It wasn't perfect, but she had support and she was convinced that she could pull through.

Samantha and Faith walked through the exit doors. Faith's heart skipped a beat when she saw Tina waiting for her. Samantha turned to Faith with a smile. "Good luck out there. You're going to do fine."

Faith went to hug the nurse that had been there from the beginning. "Thank you for everything. You were amazing."

Samantha walked away leaving Faith with Tina. "Well, ya look a lot better than before. I can actually see a spark in your eye. Hadn't seen that since I met ya."

"I feel better. Feel like I have a clearer understanding of what's going on with me."

Tina jingled her car keys. "Good, now we need to sit down and look at those demons of yours, but what do you need to do first?"

Faith followed Tina outside and to her car. "I literally have no idea."

Tina unlocked the car and motioned for Faith to get in. "First thing you're going to do is call your lawyer and set up a time to see her. Next, you're going to put out more job applications. Then, once your kids get out of school, you're going to call them."

"When are we going to sit down and look at why I'm so messed up?"

"I'm available tonight? You?"

"Yes, I am. I'm ready to handle this once and for all."

Tina turned down the car radio. "Whoa there cowgirl, this isn't a one-time thing and you're done. It's a lifetime process. What we are gonna do is identify the demons, so you can start learning how to get rid of them."

Faith looked at Tina while she drove. "Whatever it takes. I'm willing to do whatever it takes."

"It's about time."

Tina drove Faith home and dropped her off. "I'll expect a phone call around 7 telling me you are on your way to my house. That should give you plenty of time to do the things I told you to do."

Faith opened the car door to get out. "Okay, I'll call you then. Bye."

"Bye."

Faith unlocked her front door and walked into her empty house that was overflowing with memories. She hated being there. She felt trapped in a nightmare when she was there. She couldn't wait for the house sale to go through. She was perfectly fine living in an apartment while she looked for somewhere else to live.

First thing she did was call her lawyer. "Good afternoon, this is the office of Mrs. McNair. How may I help you?"

Nervous energy coursed through Faith. "Uh, this is Faith Smith. I had to miss an appointment with Mrs. McNair and was calling to reschedule."

"Of course. You were scheduled to see her last week, correct?"

"Yes."

"She has an opening for tomorrow morning at 9:30. Is that a good time?"

"Yes, of course."

"Okay, I have you on the schedule. Make sure you arrive about 15 minutes early to fill out some paperwork."

"I'll be there."

Faith hung up the phone and checked her email for any responses to her job applications that she had filled out before her stint in the hospital. To her surprise there was a response from a local grocery store asking her for an interview. She immediately filled out the online form to schedule an interview for the following afternoon and decided to apply to other grocery stores just in case this one didn't pan out.

Well that's that. I did what I was told to do. Now I just have to wait to call my kids.

Faith waited the hour to call her kids. She wasn't sure what to say, or how they would react. So, she sat and waited in silence thinking about how she was going to tell them what had happened. God only knew what Matt had told them. When the hour was up, she reached for the phone and put in Matt's number.

She hoped that he would know that she was calling the kids and would let them answer, but she wasn't surprised when he answered the phone. "Hello. What do you want?"

"Well hello to you too. I just want to talk with the kids."

"So, you're out of the hospital again? Tried to kill yourself this time? Why would you do that? Did you even think of the kids? Of course not. All you ever do is think about yourself."

Fighting back the anger that was swelling in her gut, Faith answered. "I don't want to do this with you. I didn't call to talk to you. I called to talk with the kids. Put them on the phone."

"Whatever. Athena your mom is on the phone."

"Hey, Mom! Are you out of the hospital?"

"Yes, I am baby. Sorry I had to leave you so abruptly."

"Is it true what I've been hearing that you were going to jump off the bridge?"

"Where did you hear that from?"

"Dad and Martha were talking about it and I overheard."

Anger began to boil within her gut, but this time she didn't feel the need to give into it. Maybe it was the medicine, or the fact that she didn't need more trouble that kept her in check. She didn't care which it was. She was just grateful that whatever it was was working.

Faith took a deep breath. "Yes, baby, it's true."

Desperation filled Faith's ears. "But, why would you do that? Why would you leave us without you?"

"I allowed someone to convince me that y'all were better off without me."

"Mom, that's the stupidest thing I've ever heard. We love you and don't want anything to happen to you. Please, Mom never think that again."

"Okay, baby, I won't. I'm sorry to have scared you. How was your week?"

"It was fine. Just the same thing of going to school. When can we see you?"

"I'm not sure. I'll have to arrange that with your dad. How are Michael and Mary?"

"Annoying as ever, but fine."

"Are they home?"

"No, they're at soccer practice."

Faith's heart sank. "Oh, okay. Maybe I'll call back later. Can you tell them I called?"

"Sure."

"I love you."

"I love you too Mom."

"Bye, baby."

"Bye."

Faith hung up the phone. She didn't want to risk Matt getting back on the phone. She was too angry to talk to him. How could he talk about her trip to the hospital with Martha? He seemed to talk to her about everything and some of it wasn't true. She was sick of him and of Martha.

Time passed with Faith cleaning the house and throwing out more stuff she didn't need and didn't want. She enjoyed purging the dead weight. She was starting a new chapter in her life and didn't want to be consumed with the burdens of her old life. As soon as she had the money from the sale of the house she was moving out. She couldn't wait.

The time had come for her to call Tina. She dialed in her number and waited for her to answer. "Hey there. Get everything done?"

"Sure did. I see the lawyer tomorrow morning and I have a job interview tomorrow afternoon."

"Good deal. Well, come on over and let's get down to business."

"On my way."

Faith drove over to Tina's listening to music with the windows down. She was ready to face everything. She pulled into Tina's driveway confident that whatever they were going to do was going to be her first real steps towards freedom.

Tina was waiting for her in the garage. "You ready to get this started?"

"Yes I am."

"Good. Let's start at the beginning. I asked you this question months ago, but I don't think you answered it as truthfully as you should have. Do you admit you're an alcoholic? You can have no reservations on this. The only way to deal with a problem is to admit you have one."

Faith hesitated. Deep down she knew she was an alcoholic, but she kept falling back onto the fact that Matt kept saying she wasn't except in the custody battle. She didn't want to be an alcoholic because that meant she could never drink again, and drinking was all she ever knew. Drinking was her solution to everything. How was she supposed to live without alcohol?

"Faith? Why do you hesitate?"

She snapped out of her thoughts. "I...I don't know how to live."

Tina sighed. "We all know that feeling, but trust me life is more beautiful without it. You just have to learn the tools to overcome the harder parts of life. Now, are you an alcoholic or not?"

Faith looked into Tina's dark brown eyes and for the first time since she started this journey she was willing and able to admit her problem. "Yes. Yes, I am."

"Now we can get down to business. Tell me everything you are angry about and have a resentment towards."

"I'm not really an angry person and I don't hold grudges, so I don't know how to do what you ask."

Tina's laughter hurt Faith's ears. "You don't have anger, or hold a grudge? Tell me then how did you wind up with an assault and battery charge? Tell me about those fights with Matt. What about the cousin you beat up? A person at peace doesn't go around beating people up. A person who doesn't hold grudges doesn't get into verbal fights with anyone that will participate."

A moment passed with Faith sitting in shocked silence. It was true. She did do those things, but that was because those people deserved it. They hurt her. "Ok, so I was angry, but I don't hold resentments."

Tina lit a cigarette. "What about Martha? You never have anything nice to say about Martha."

"That's different she is a mean hateful person. I told you what she said to me. She basically said I was better off dead. I...I just can't with her. I would love to put her in her place. She thinks her shit doesn't stink, but whenever I see her, or think of her it's all I can see. A great big pile of shit."

"That's a resentment. What would you say to her if you had the chance?"

"What I want to say and what I should say are two different realities?"

"Why? If she deserves it then what's holding you back?"

"To say what I think would get me into trouble with everyone I know."

Tina crossed her legs letting her eyes bore into Faith. "Humor me."

"Ok. I want to look her dead straight in the eyes, unleash the demon that I have chained up, and call her out on her hypocrisy, on her bullshit."

"So, pretend I'm her and tell me what you would say."

Faith took a deep breath and unlocked the chains that bound her demon from Martha for so many months. She felt him rattling free, felt that tide of fury flow to her fingertips, felt that animalistic hunter moving in for the kill.

"You are a vile, hate filled hypocrite who thrives on dominating with furious tyranny over anyone who dares to cross you. You relish your throne that you sit yourself on and look down on people who you think are wrong for whatever reason. You sit on your throne and act like you do no wrong when in fact you are the worst of the worst kind of people. You do not know compassion, nor mercy, nor love. All you know is yourself seeking desire to be better than others. You do not know joy. You only know the feeling of justified vengeance. You relish in the tormenting of others. I've seen how you gossip about people. I've been there when you tore someone down when they pissed you off. You seek to uplift yourself by standing on the carcass of anyone you believe inferior. You're a miserable bitch who cares for no one, forgives no one, truly loves no one. You love only those that serve a purpose and once that purpose is served you destroy them. Love does not exist in you, only hate! Love and hate do not coexist. It's either one or the other, and you have chosen to murder with your words and actions. You are evil and you will be the one who dies alone surrounded only by your vengeful hate."

Tina put out her cigarette. "Feel better?"

"Kinda. I want to say all of that to her freaking face."

"What good would it serve? Would it change her mind, her ways?"

Faith let out a deep sigh. "No, I don't suppose it would."

"Is saying these things something God would want?"

Another deep sigh. "No, of course not."

Tina's dark eyes once again pierced into Faith. "What part did you play in her anger?"

"What the hell do you mean, 'what part did I play?' She came after me. She told me that my kids were better off without me!"

"So, she just said those things out of nowhere. You did nothing to spark her anger?"

Faith looked down at her hands, hating the answer to her question. "I guess I hurt her, but I don't deserve what she has done. She has spread lies and gossip about me. She has said hurtful things."

Tina shrugged her shoulders. "So? How is it your business what she thinks, or does? That is between her and her God. She is God's business not yours."

Tina lit another cigarette, exhaled the white smoke, and looked into Faith's eyes. "Look honestly into the mirror. Why are you really mad at Martha?"

Faith knew why. The answer hit her while she vomited her own hate. Vocalizing that answer was not something she desired to do. Put into words another could hear would give life to the reality she wanted so desperately to run from. But, running was something she had always done and now she had run herself into a ditch with no way out except to exit the vehicle of denial, turn around, and crawl back to the road she had veered from. Faith lit her own cigarette unable to deny its beckoning.

"I'm not mad at her. I'm mad at myself. I'm not saying those things to her; I'm saying those things to myself. I'm using her to deflect my feelings, my responsibilities. Truth is I hurt her. I hurt a lot of people because I hated myself. In many ways I still do."

And there it was. The truth. She hated herself and always had. A gentle tide of relief spread over Faith. She was, for the first time in her life, looking at the stranger in the mirror. All her life she had hated that stranger, but now Faith was beginning to see that she was just as unfair to her as she was to the other people around her. Tiny tears slid down her cheek. She brushed them away.

Tina moved to the edge of her seat placing herself only inches away from Faith. "Who would you say is your master?"

Confused Faith drew on her cigarette and exhaled. "God?"

"Is this God of yours loving?"

Faith's voice quivered. "Yes."

"Is he forgiving?"

Shifting in her seat unable to get comfortable, Faith answered. "Yes."

"Have you acknowledged your wrongs and made amends where you could?"

"Yes."

Tina put out her cigarette. "You sure that you have made amends everywhere you could?"

A tiny thought creeped into Faith's mind. It was a thought she most definitely did not want to pursue, but knew that Tina would keep pressing. "Maybe not everywhere I could."

Her knowing eyes pushed upon Faith's skull as she looked at her well-manicured nails. Tina pushed. "Where do you need to clean house?"

Faith paused. She fidgeted with her fingers then tugged and twirled her hair. She didn't want to answer because she didn't want to ever make an amends to that one person who had hurt her so deeply. "With Martha?"

"Exactly. You need to make your amends to her. You failed at your job causing her to have to work harder. You took a trust you had with her and threw it away when you beat the hell outta that woman."

Faith rebuked. "But she has said and done horrible things to me!"

Tina locked her gaze upon Faith. "So have you. What does love demand?"

"Creation?"

"And when that creation is wrong, does your God seek to punish?"

"No, he seeks to forgive."

"So, your God is forgiving of you?"

Faith sighed. She knew where this was going. "Yes."

"So, he is forgiving of Martha?"

She couldn't hide the disgust in her voice. Faith muttered. "Yes."

Faith looked up to the blue sky. "Yes. I get your point."

"You said he is your master. Do we not do as the Master commands?"

Disgust furrowed Faith's eyebrows and it was all she could do to not roll her eyes. "So, I have to forgive and ask her forgiveness?"

Tina shifted in her seat. "Which master do you want to serve? Your God, or yourself? Do you want to know love, or hate?"

"I want love."

"Then do what love demands. Forgive her and forgive yourself. Reach out the hand of apology and clean your house."

Faith chuckled. "She is liable to cut it off."

"Can you blame her? Besides if she does, that is her right. Again none of your business. Your only business is to keep your hands clean."

"Fine. I'll apologize."

"What about Matt?"

"What about him?"

"Are you going to tell me you don't have a resentment towards him? Remember to be honest with yourself."

"Hell-yes I have a resentment towards him. He has put me through hell for years. His constant belittling me, the fights, and now how he is using the kids to get back at me. He is an ass."

"Again, what part did you play?"

Anger filled Faith. She balled one hand into a fist while the other hand grabbed at a cigarette and lit it. "I may not be innocent, but I didn't deserve half of what he did to me."

"Nor did he deserve half of what you did to him. You were a drunk for your whole marriage. You picked fights with him. You left him to care for the kids while you had not one, but two breakdowns. You're not innocent in how things went down."

This time Faith rolled her eyes and spoke through gritted teeth. "Oh, you have got to be kidding me. I have to apologize to him too?"

Tina tilted her head upwards and continued in spite of Faith's dirty look. "Do you want freedom?"

"Of course, but—"

Tina shook her finger back and forth. "But, nothing. Freedom isn't free. It has a price and the price here is accepting your part in how things went down. You could have chosen a much different path that wouldn't have led to this mess you're in, but you chose the current path you're on. Now you can stay on that path and stay miserable and eventually go back to drinking, or you can do something about it. Do the next right thing that your higher power would have you do.

"This isn't about what you want. It's about what's right."

Faith sat in silence watching the smoke float in the air. "I'm not as innocent as I once thought."

"Of course not. None of us are. Sure, we like to live in this bubble that says we are as pure as the driven snow, but the truth is that we are all fallen creatures that screw up."

"But, why do I have to face that and someone like Martha never will?"

Tina leaned back allowing her arms to rest on her legs. "Because for you, if you don't, you'll die."

Faith turned her head to watch a car drive by the house wishing she was in that car instead of doing this crap with Tina. "Oh."

Tina's eyes filled with compassion. "Is Martha really happy? Is Matt?"

A deep moan escaped Faith. She could see where Tina's question was leading to and she didn't like how it made her feel sympathy for people just minutes ago she wanted to curse to hell. "I don't see how you can be happy and be that vengeful."

Tina leaned into Faith and placed her hand on her knee. "Exactly. Happy people don't go around gossiping and saying messed up shit. They live and let live. Happy people forgive even when forgiveness isn't asked for. Happy people don't lash out at others. They aren't happy. That's sad for them. Now, do you want to be happy, or do you want to play the victim for the rest of your life?"

Faith relaxed into the chair. She was tired of fighting the truth. "I want to be happy."

"So, go apologize for your part in things. May I suggest that you do that tomorrow? The faster you do it, the better off you'll be."

"Okay."

"From here on out you need to see your part in every situation. Once you see your part you'll know a certain freedom. Constantly playing the victim is exhausting and deprives you of living life."

Faith shook her head. "I don't like the sound of always knowing my part, but I understand why it's important."

"Remember the point is not whether or not, you like it. It's about what is right. Always do the next right thing no matter how you feel about it."

"Will do. I'm going to go home and get some rest."

Tina rose from her chair. "Good. You need to rest. You have a lot of work to do. Let me know what you plan on saying when you apologize."

Faith rose to her feet and fumbled with her keys. "I will. Bye."

Tina gently grabbed Faith's arm. "You're not leaving without a hug. You did good work today. Be easy on yourself."

Faith melted into Tina. "Thank you. Thank you for everything."

Tina watched as Faith got into her car. "No problem. Just remember, one day you will be able to help someone who is dying in their addiction."

Faith smiled and started the car. *How could I ever help anyone? I'm a freaking mess.*

She pulled out of the driveway and began the drive home. *Maybe Tina is right. Maybe one day I will be better and can use this disaster of a life I have now to help someone out. That will be a good day.*

CAROL SAT WATCHING FAITH. Faith noticed that her appearance seemed lighter. The dark contours of her face began to reflect some light. Her once dead eyes appeared to have a tiny spark of light in them. Carol straightened herself in her seat. "Did you apologize to Martha and Matt?"

Faith smiled. "I did. It wasn't easy. No one likes apologizing to someone who has done their fair share of wrong, but I have a program and I am responsible to that program to do the action needed for me to stay sober."

"Did it piss you off to have to say sorry to them?"

"Absolutely. All I could see was the wrongs they had done and how screwed up their actions had been, but what I was taught was that it wasn't my place to judge what others did or didn't do. My place was to look at what I did or didn't do that needed correcting."

Carol shook her head. "It doesn't seem fair. If you've been wronged then why should you have to apologize. I don't get it."

"Everyone is flawed. Everyone needs a program. Some people find their program in religion, or in karma. Some find it in a group of drunks. Wherever you find it you will find that you have to look at yourself and work on your defects. Those who don't are doomed to live a life of misery. They will never be happy. They'll have bouts of happiness, but they have no true joy. They wear the chains of selfishness to their death. I don't want to be that person anymore if that means I have to apologize to a jerk then that's what I do. People like you and me don't have a choice. We either do the action, or we fall into that alcohol drug abyss of which there is no survival."

Carol frowned. "I don't like it."

Faith chuckled. "You sound like a kid having to eat their vegetables. As I was told, I will tell you. It's not about what you like. It's about what is right. Doing the right thing often means setting yourself to the side for the good of others. Doing good for others is ultimately where we find our joy, our freedom."

"If you say so. How did they take your apologies?"

Faith snickered. "Exactly the way I thought they would. They accepted the apology followed by a litany of words justifying how they behaved. They were the poor victim in everything. But, I left each one feeling more empowered than I had when I walked in. I owned my part. My hands were washed clean. I didn't need to grovel and beg for mercy. I don't do that anymore. I stand with my head held high and if I owe an amends then I make an amends and move on. I know who I am today, and I am proud of that person today.

Tears burned Carol's eyes. "I want that. To be proud of who I am no matter what. I don't know what that's like."

She wiped away her tears. That tiny spec of light flickered as if about to blow out. Her lips turned down and she began to hang her head under the weight of what was coming next.

Faith held Carol's hand. She, better than anyone, understood how heavy the burden was to realize sobriety is not an overnight matter. "You can have it. Just do the next right thing and over time you will piece together the person your creator wants you to be."

Carol shook her head and quickly wiped away the tears that were now streaming down her cheeks. "You make it sound so easy."

"It is simple, but it's not easy. The battle within regenerates with each sunrise. One side wants to call out by name those who have lied, those who have lifted their tongues to slither around my neck to choke out all life. Make no mistake that dark part of me wants blood. I want to see them drown in the filth they churned up. The other side, however, will walk away from the horde of ravenous dogs and let them choke on the carcass of their lives. I will carry on. I will rise above. I will live life as I see fit under the direction of my higher power."

"Won't that mean being alone? I'm afraid of being alone." Carol fidgeted with her fingers.

Faith rested her back on the chair she had called home for the last several hours. "Once upon a time I was afraid of being alone because I didn't like me. I'm not afraid of standing alone anymore. If alone I must be then alone I will be, but I refuse to lay myself on the altar to appease a community of hypocrites. No longer will I lay on my back and be devoured by monsters rattling against the prison of their deceits."

Carol looked into Faith's eyes. "My past is filled with people I've wronged and things I'm ashamed of. How can I move on from that? What God would have me?"

Faith's smile was one of recognition. She understood perfectly what Carol was asking, for she had asked the same questions. Faith moved her chair closer to Carol and leaned in close. Her hand gently grabbed Carol's slumped shoulder. "The past is the most difficult to overcome. The person you were and the sins you committed will revisit your memories ensnaring you into a downward spiral of self-pity and self- hatred. There will always be people who will never let you forget. They will curse your name and throw traps in your path in the hope that they will forever capture you in their claws. They see no flaw in themselves. They acknowledge no sin. They forever claim victimhood. But you must avoid these traps. They are sick the same as you are. They have inflicted their sin onto others. They are as much a villain as they have made you out to be. Leave them to God for he loves them the same as he loves you. He will hold them accountable just as he has done with you. Worry not about your past. Clean up where you can and leave the rest to God. Be bold, be proud, be happy, and life will carry new meaning."

Hundreds of people had come and gone in the coffee shop. Some had looked over at Faith and Carol with curiosity. Most, however, had not even noticed them. People come and people go. What their own stories are; no one really knows. Carol tucked a strand of hair behind her ear. More tears gathered and fell from her eyes. "Do you ever have days that you want to give up and just go back to the way things were?"

Faith softly nodded her head. She was careful to keep her

focus on Carol who was on the edge of a cliff. "Absolutely, but on those days I remember that I cannot give up. I cannot give in. No matter who. No matter what. I will not lay down and die. To go back is to dig my own grave that will reach out and break my sanity before it breaks my body. I will grab God's hand, pull myself up and keep going forward. Are there people who want to see me fail? Yeap, but to hell with them. I don't live for them. I live for me. Today I walk my own path following the will of my creator. Today I stand tall against the onslaught of hate. Tomorrow I will rise up and be the person God wants me to be."

Faith paused for a moment allowing Carol to absorb what she had said and handed her a napkin to dry her eyes. "Today, I look to the skies and fly with the birds. I spread my wings and catch the winds of happiness. Sometimes the crosswinds threaten to throw me off course, but today I know how to fly."

Carol leaned away from Faith and for the first time since she arrived looked around the coffee shop at all the people rushing here and there. She rubbed the napkin across her eyes and then wiped her nose. "I want to be happy like these people are. I want to have a life." Carol let her head drop down.

Faith leaned in towards Carol unwilling to let her back away. Her hand brushed against her chin and lifted her head up. "You can be happy and have a life, or you can stay on the course you're on and die. The choice is yours. Which path are you going to take?"

Carol's shoulders began to shake as the sobs broke through her tough exterior. She was done. She was broken. "You'll be with me?"

Quickly, Faith wiped away a tear that had fallen. "Absolutely. You never have to be alone again."

EPILOGUE

Faith started her SUV and called her dear friend. "Hey girl, how did it go?"

"Hey, Tina. I think it went well. She wants to be sober."

"How do you feel?"

Faith paused for a brief moment. "I feel good. It feels good to actually help someone."

Tina's voice echoed through the phone. "I told you that one day your mess would be able to help someone else. Believe me now?"

Faith chuckled. "Yes, I do. We still on for dinner?"

"Absolutely."

"Great. Talk to ya then."

"Okay."

Faith hung up the phone and began driving back to her condo. Three years had passed since she first took that chip. Faith thought about all that she had been through during those years. *I have come a long way. Thank God I am no longer in that dark place.*

She pulled into the parking space in front of her two story condo that she had purchased with her boyfriend of two years.

She sat there for a moment looking at the brick home. Waiting inside for her was Paul and Mary. Paul was sober like her and she had always been drawn to him even during the early months of sobriety. He was her rock, her best friend, her soulmate.

Faith's heart swelled as she thought of Mary. Mary had decided to live with her instead of Matt. Faith was beyond grateful to have at least one of her children back in her life. Athena and Michael still lived with Matt, but Faith had hurt them deeply and only time and right action would heal her relationship with them. Her heart ached for them. She saw them regularly, but knowing she had hurt them caused her pain.

She gathered her things and went inside. "Mommy!"

Smiling Faith went to grab Mary. "Hey baby, whatcha doing?"

Bouncing around the living room, Mary laughed. "I just won at my game that I have been playing all day. How did your meeting go?"

Putting her purse away, Faith went to the kitchen where Paul was waiting for her with a steaming cup of chamomile tea. "It went well. I think I actually helped her."

Paul smiled at her. "Good. I'm proud of you."

Faith brushed her hand through Paul's black hair and leaned in for a kiss. "Thank you. Never thought I would be in a position to help anyone."

Faith took the tea and went upstairs to get ready for dinner with Tina. Paul called after her. "Don't forget to call Sam back."

"Oh yeah. Thanks." Faith grabbed her phone and called her boss Sam. He was an amazing boss who had given her her first job in Drug and Alcohol Counseling. "Hey, thanks for calling me back. I just wanted to make sure that you were ready to lead the training on Monday."

Faith smiled. "Yes, I am. I've been ready for a week. I think it's going to be an amazing training if I do say so myself."

"Good. Glad to hear. Have a good evening."

"You too."

Faith hung up the phone and looked into the bathroom mirror. She finally knew the woman staring back at her. *I know you. You're looking good.*

Yes, I am.

We've come a hell of a long way.

Yes, we have.

I love you.

The woman staring at her smiled. *It's about time.*

ACKNOWLEDGMENTS

First and foremost, I would like to thank God who has always had my back even when I turned it on him. I would like to thank my partner in life, Richard, for your never ending support. To my parents, for standing by me through the storms, thank you. To my editor Griffin Smith for helping me take this book to the next level and helping a dream become reality, thank you.

AUTHOR PAGE

Sheree Coleman lives in Houston, TX with her partner, children, and a crazy cat. She is a former teacher who has always had a passion for writing. She has a flare for the dramatic, especially when it comes to flying roaches. She uses this flare to fuel her novel *Surviving Hell*.

Lightning Source UK Ltd.
Milton Keynes UK
UKHW040827230322
400493UK00001B/257